MICHAEL L. CARL, M.D.

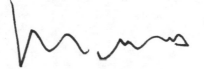

BLESSINGS OF A
FAITHFUL MAN

TATE PUBLISHING
AND ENTERPRISES, LLC

Published by Tate Publishing & Enterprises, LLC
127 E. Trade Center Terrace | Mustang, Oklahoma 73064 USA
1.888.361.9473 | www.tatepublishing.com

Tate Publishing is committed to excellence in the publishing industry. The company reflects the philosophy established by the founders, based on Psalm 68:11,
"The Lord gave the word and great was the company of those who published it."

Book design copyright © 2011 by Tate Publishing, LLC. All rights reserved.
Cover design by Joel Uber
Interior design by Kenna Davis

Published in the United States of America

ISBN: 978-1-61346-742-8
1. Religion / Christian Life / Inspirational
2. Religion / Christian Life / Family
11.10.10

DEDICATION

This book is lovingly dedicated to all of my family and friends who have been such a guiding force and an inspiration in my life. May God bless you and keep you all the days of your lives.

ACKNOWLEDGEMENTS

I want to offer my heartfelt thanks to the entire editing staff at Tate Publications, especially Janey Hays my acquisition editor, and Jenn Scott, my conceptual editor. All of their suggestions and help in writing this story were invaluable to producing the final book.

I also need to mention my eternal gratitude to my personal editor and daughter-in-law, Michelle (Miller) Carl. Michelle is the Managing Editor of the Roseville Press Tribune newspaper, and helped immensely in organizing and composing drafts and re-drafts of the final manuscript.

Thank you to all of these great editors and any one else who read the original draft and provided feedback.

TABLE OF CONTENTS

PROLOGUE

This is a story that had to be written. Not because it is a mystery, although some might say, myself included, that many of the events in the story qualify as mysteries in and of themselves. And not because it's an enthralling adventure tale, even though it has been an incredible lifelong journey that hasn't ended yet. No, this is a story that must be told for one reason only: because God told me to tell it.

Now, reading that last line, you might think, "Oh no. Another religious fanatic trying to convert me." You might also think, "I just wasted the cost of this book that I will never read," and then throw it away. My hope, however, is that you will stick with it and finish it if for no other reason than to see if it touches you in some way or another on a level beyond the monotonous routine of our daily lives. If it does touch you on some higher level, then I've accomplished everything I set out to do. And if you do stick with the story and finish the book, I promise that at the end, you should have a clear idea of why God told me to write this story.

I have never been a religious zealot in my life and have never been compelled to push my beliefs on others around me. In fact, the few times that others have force—fed me the rigid version of why their particular beliefs are the only road to the Higher Creator, I usually have turned away and done my utmost to avoid them in the future. I am reminded of one particularly difficult position my wife Susan and I were put into at the beginning of 1995. Our son David was a senior and was halfway through his final year of high school. He had met a new girlfriend at the start of school and was quickly developing a heavy relationship with her. Her parents were interested in meeting us and invited us to a "gathering of friends" on January 2. This just happens to be my wife's birthday. Instead of celebrating it in the way she would rather mark the day, we were meeting David's girlfriend's parents, along with their group of friends, none of whom we knew or had met in the past. It turned out this gathering was a regular Sunday afternoon prayer group that met at their house. They were members of an ultra—conservative Christian church in our hometown of Davis, California. Apparently, these regular meetings were used by leaders assigned by the pastor of the congregation to ensure that none of the members were straying from their commitment to God and the church. The leader for this day's group meeting saw us come in the front door and, recognizing we were strangers to the group, immediately pounced on us to find out who we were and why we were there. He quickly asked if we believed in Jesus and had a strong Christian faith life. Caught by utter surprise, I replied, "Well, yes. We are Catholic Christians and have been since our son David was born." After being told that Catholics are not really true Christians, we were invited to have a seat in the living room and proceeded to be grilled about our belief in Jesus and any true faith experiences we had been through. I spoke about some of our beliefs and experiences only to be criticized for having been baptized as a baby at a time when I had no knowledge of accepting Jesus Christ as my Savior and path to God. Realizing this was a no—win situation, I muttered thanks under my breath that it was Susan's birthday. I deftly excused us from this very interesting conversation since we had early reservations for a romantic dinner. To this day, I regret that we left our son to fend for himself in a den of Christian lions. David did, however, have his girlfriend to appease the carnivores by calming the pride with her promises of his eventual conversion to their righteous ways. Needless to say, David's relationship with her ended about six months later, and we have had no further contact with the girlfriend or the family!

Despite my lack of a burning need to lead everyone around me to Catholicism, I have usually been open to talking about my beliefs and faith when asked by others. There has always been a strong thread of that faith that has weaved its way through every event and experience in my life. This thread of faith was first embedded in the fabric of my being when my mother and grandparents shared their love of God and family with me as the newest member of their clan. Like a guiding path, it has led me to each chapter and turn in the road as my journey has unfolded.

I have tried, as an adult, to let my actions and relationships with others be my examples of living the faith rather than spouting words of conversion. Saint Francis of Assisi once said, "Preach the gospel at all times, and when necessary, use words." Of course, this has been much easier said than done. I have often found myself disappointed in the way I acted in a particular situation or the words I used with a family member or acquaintance when I looked back in reflection. The key has been to be willing to apologize and try to do better the next time. I have found that things go much better in life situations and relationships when I have used love, patience, and compassion to guide my actions rather than ego, spite, or anger.

EARLY YEARS

I spent the first four years of life growing up in the Imperial Valley, a massive center of agriculture and livestock located east of San Diego in Southern California. The valley is essentially reclaimed desert developed over the last century using the waters of the mighty Colorado River that flows south to the Gulf of California. The crops that are raised in the valley are sustained through an elaborate network of canals and irrigation ditches. My grandparents lived east of the small town of Calipatria, or Calipat as it is often called by its residents and other valley locals. Calipat sits 180 feet below sea level in the middle of the valley, and one of its claims to fame is the world's tallest flagpole, the tip of which reaches sea level. My grandparents lived in a company house that sat on the western bank of the High Line Canal. My grandfather was a zanjero, Spanish for ditch worker. He was employed by the Imperial Irrigation District and spent his days driving through the thriving agricultural fields and releasing measured amounts of precious water into the acres of crops. I can fondly remember being a three—year—old riding in his pickup truck with him and watching as he sent the liquid gold flowing through metal gates that blocked the entrance to each field's irrigation channels. I was very close to my grandparents growing up as a toddler and fondly called my grandfather DaDa. He was the major father figure in my life at that time. He would come home at lunch every day and lay down with me for a nap before returning to his irrigation duties. My grandmother was the main babysitter for my mother, as she was working full time at the Calipatria High School office. Grandma, as I called her, was always hugging me and saying, "Give me sugar," as she would kiss me on my neck. She really enjoyed games and activities and was always teaching me some new trick, craft, or game. We would work puzzles together, do simple math problems, and bake cookies as a treat. I never had any doubt that my Grandma's love was genuine and never ending.

Grandma's father, John Howland, was the last member of the family who was a registered member of the Cherokee nation. His mother, Susan Rider, had walked the Trail of Tears from the Carolina Cherokee Nation's native lands to the newly established Cherokee reservation in Northeast Oklahoma. My grandma was born on the reservation and was never issued a birth certificate. This made it very difficult later in my life, after Grandma had died, when I wanted to establish my own link to the Cherokee nation for the posterity of the family. I was able to accomplish it with certified letters from two of my great aunts attesting that Grandma was the daughter of John Howland. It was because of this family heritage that my Grandma would playfully threaten to send me back to the Indians on the reservation whenever I was acting out or disobeying her. Life was a simpler time in my early years during the mid to late 1950s. The company house did have a telephone, although it was on a party line. You often might pick it up to make a call and find that a neighbor was using the line and would either shorten their call or ask you to wait to make your outgoing call. My earliest recollection was that the kitchen had an icebox for food storage. My grandpa would drop by the ice house every other day or so and pick up a block of ice to cool the box. We did eventually move to an early version of a refrigerator, but nothing close to today's models with ice dispensers, water in the door, and side—by—side freezers. Laundry was done in a wringer washer and hung on the clothesline outside to dry. There was also a sheet metal washtub that doubled as a play pool for me during the sweltering days of spring and summer in the valley.

During those early years of childhood, my mother and I lived in a two bedroom cottage just north of Main Street in Calipat. It was an old concrete and stucco building in a row of about six or seven similar cottages. Believe it or not, the old house was still standing and occupied when I passed through the town a few years ago. Most of my time, however, was spent out at the house on the canal. I have loving memories of bonfires and weenie roasts and making homemade ice cream with an old, hand—cranked ice cream maker.

My grandparents attended the Methodist church in Calipat, and I remember going with Grandma to rummage sales there as a toddler. My mother also attended the Methodist church and sang in the 11:00 a.m. choir every Sunday. It didn't seem to be enough for her, and she felt as though she was searching for something more in her faith journey. She went to the Catholic Church in Brawley a few times with a friend and found that Catholicism provided what her soul was yearning for, so she converted to the faith. She continued to sing in the choir at the Methodist church each Sunday after going to the early morning mass beforehand. After I was born, she and I began attending mass at the small Saint Patrick's Catholic Church in Calipat. I was baptized at this small church as an infant and still have an old photograph of my godparents, Mr. and Mrs. Riley, holding me in a white baptism outfit and wrapped in a white blanket.

Missing from my memories of these early times in my life was any recollection of my father. It wasn't until I was almost four years old that a stranger showed up at the old cottage we lived in and was introduced to me as my father. It wasn't clear to me until many years later why there was this unknown gap in my early childhood relationship with my father. I was aware as I grew into an older child that he had served in the US Army during the Korean War. I presumed that this was the explanation for the gap in those years.

Shortly after my father entered my life, we moved to another, bigger house west of the airport that sat on the western outskirts of Calipat. We lived there for a short time and then moved to a house my parents purchased in Brawley, a larger town that sits roughly ten miles south of Calipat. Brawley is the location of Pioneer's Memorial Hospital, the place of my birth. By the time I turned five, my father had been hired for a new position in the accounting department of General Atomics, a company located in the small junction of Torrey Pines, just north of San Diego proper. Shortly after we moved, my parents purchased a house in Kearny Mesa, a new suburb of San Diego on the northern borders of the city that was spreading eastward from the existing neighborhood of Clairemont.

It was here where I spent the majority of my childhood and met one of my best friends I have ever known, a fellow five—year—old, Larry, who lived across the street from us. Today, Larry and I continue to share a lifelong bond and have supported each other through many good times and many times of hardship.

Despite our new home in San Diego, the ties to the Imperial Valley persisted in our life. My mother and I would make frequent trips down to visit family and friends as well as continuing to use the same family doctors for care. She returned to Pioneer's Memorial Hospital to deliver my new little sister, Lisa. It was always so comforting for me to go home to the old company house on the highline and receive so much love and attention from my grandparents. They lived there until my grandpa retired from the Irrigation District, at which time they moved over to the San Diego area in the small community of Santee. This was a comfortable area for them, as it was semi—rural with farms and ranches. The weather east of San Diego is also much warmer, not receiving the ocean influence of breezes and marine layer clouds.

Life in the late fifties and early sixties continued to be simple and easy to live. We didn't have a lot of money for extravagances, but playing with Larry and the rest of the neighborhood kids was all I needed. The two of us attended elementary school together, sharing the same teachers for kindergarten, first grade, and part of second grade. It was that last year when a new school opened several miles away and our street was the dividing line for attendance. Halfway through the second grade, Larry began to attend Charles A. Lindbergh Elementary School and I stayed on at Pete W. Ross School. It was a difficult split, but we continued our fast friendship in the after school and weekend hours.

The hardest impact Larry and I experienced in our friendship occurred at the end of the third grade. Larry's father was a naval officer and was deployed for three years to Japan. The prospect of Larry moving all the way to Japan was untenable, and we made plans to run away from home and live as friends in Colorado. The minds of two eight—year—olds could concoct numerous unrealistic and impossible schemes, but we truly believed we could ride our bicycles from California to Colorado and survive on animals killed with my BB gun. Fortunately, my parents caught us in the middle of the night, preparing our equipment and bicycles, and put a swift end to our crazy notion. Larry did move for the three years to Japan; and when he returned to San Diego, I had developed new friendships that were difficult to integrate another person into easily. My new best friend who lived next door and attended my junior high school, Bill, didn't like Larry and seemed to do his best to alienate him from our tight, little, two—person friendship. As Bill moved on in his life and out of mine, Larry continued to treasure our friendship. I realize how mean and hateful we had been to Larry during those hard couple of years.

The whole area of Kearny Mesa and Clairemont was expanding rapidly as San Diego moved from a sleepy navy town south of Los Angeles to a burgeoning metropolis with its own infrastructure and business economy. Consequently, Larry and I attended different junior and senior high schools, causing us to put our friendship on hold for several years. As is often true in life, we went our separate paths and developed new relationships and priorities. However, our friendship was still intact, albeit not as frequent or tight. Larry pursued motorcycles and cars, and I was learning to surf in my spare time during high school. True, lasting friendships will endure such times, and ours certainly did, continuing to be very strong to this day.

THE LOVE OF MY LIFE

In 1971, I was living the life of a typical San Diego teen: attending high school, surfing, working part—time at a McDonald's restaurant, and partying with friends. I experimented during my junior and senior high school years with various drugs, including amphetamines, barbiturates, cocaine, and marijuana. On the weekends, smoking pot and drinking was the routine activity for me and my friends as we made the rounds of football games, playing poker, or shooting pool. I have distinct memories of coming very close to being caught by the police in possession of wine and marijuana. One night, while driving my Dad's car home from a visiting football game, there were three of us guys along with three girls packed into the car, and we had been sharing a gallon jug of Spanada as well as smoking joints as we drove back to the Kearny Mesa area. At a stoplight, a VW bug filled with four boys I knew from the wrestling team pulled alongside and started harassing the girls and telling the ladies to join them in the VW. I pulled away from the light and proceeded to try to lose them in the winding streets of the neighborhood. I rounded a corner, made a quick, sharp right turn into the driveway of a house, and shut the car and the lights off. I was hoping they would drive right by, but they saw us as they made the turn and pulled alongside the curb. Within ten seconds, another set of lights pulled up along with a flashing set of police lights on top of the car. We stashed the wine bottle under several of the girls' sweaters piled on the floor and began eating the remaining pot as quickly as we could stomach it. I jumped out to talk directly with the policeman, hoping he wouldn't search the car and find the wine. He asked the usual questions about where we had been and where we were going in such a hurry. The driver of the VW was as worried as I was and timidly told him they had been chasing us in a harmless game. He told us to pack everyone up and take them home and then took off with no more questions or searches. Sometimes you just get lucky, or maybe God was looking out for us to help us avoid DUI charges and a criminal record.

Another car episode was a little more humorous but still as dangerous to my license and the use of my dad's car. Another friend of mine on the wrestling team, Brad, was accompanying me to a house where a flirtatious girl was babysitting and had called me to tell us to come by to see her. As I picked Brad up from his house, he grabbed a half—full gallon bottle of the same Spanada wine we so loved to drink and, despite his mother's protests, carried it out to my car. I told him we should place it in the trunk for safekeeping and for me not to be driving with an open container in the car. So Brad laid it on its side on the plastic mat of the trunk. When we arrived outside the location of the babysitting job, we opened the trunk and, to our horror, the gallon jug was completely empty! The cap on the bottle hadn't been tight and fell off in transit, with all of the remaining wine draining all over the plastic mat, into the spare tire well, and anywhere else it could run. We borrowed some towels from the flirtatious girl and began to frantically try to soak all of it up.

Several days later, my Dad wanted to know if one of my friends had dropped an apple core in the backseat of the car. Feigning complete ignorance, I said no and wanted to know why he was asking. "Well," he said, "there is the distinct smell of a fermented apple or some other type of fruit coming from the backseat of the car. I'll take Mom's car tomorrow, and I want you to search the car to see if anyone dropped an apple core or something behind the seat. That day, I scrubbed every inch of the trunk and the mat cover and also pulled up the floor covers in the backseat. The wine had covered every inch of the interior, and it took several hours to remove the sticky wine and the odor it was causing.

When my Dad came home from work that day, I fibbed and told him I had found the culprit: a rotting apple core, just as he had suspected. Lesson learned about transporting bottles of wine in your parents' cars!

Larry and I still occasionally had contact, but he was busy with his own circle of friends from the rival high school. In the summer after our junior year, his older sister, Debbie, was living in an apartment with a roommate. Larry wanted to have an all—night party for his friends, and Debbie agreed to allow it at her place. A couple of days prior to the Friday overnight party, Larry and I ran into each other and he extended an invitation for me to attend. It was loose and open, so I invited a friend of mine, Dale, to come with me. Dale knew Larry from the neighborhood and some teenage rock band work we had all done together in junior high school. Dale and I concocted a plan to tell our parents that we were each spending the night at the other's house. This would allow us to remain at the party all night without our parents knowing about it. We walked to the corner of my street, and Debbie picked us up in her car to take us over to the apartment. Marijuana and alcohol flowed freely at the party as more and more people arrived.

Unbeknownst to me, Larry had intentions of introducing me to one of his circle of friends, a petite girl named Kathy who wasn't attached to anyone. I was small for my age at the time, a whopping five feet two inches tall and about 100 pounds. Kathy was even shorter, at four feet ten inches, and only weighed approximately 80 pounds, so Larry envisioned the perfect match for boy and girl. However, Kathy had other plans and attended a concert with several of their acquaintances. She didn't arrive to the apartment until close to midnight, long after I had met the girl who would eventually become the love of my life.

Susan wasn't my ideal dream girl, which would have been a tan young lady with long, blonde hair— a surfer girl. However, there was something about her that really intrigued me. From the moment I first laid eyes on her, I noticed that she was full of energy and self—confidence and was very outgoing. This was completely the opposite of me, as I had been teased and harassed in my teen years due to my small size. I lacked self—confidence; was introverted around girls; and other than a few dates, never had a true, long—term relationship. Susan seemed to know with no doubts who she was and where she was going. She wore her hair in a short shag style with a dyed reddish—blonde color. She had a familiar resemblance to an actress named Sandy Duncan who, in those years, was making commercials for a bank.

I kept my intrigued eye on her but didn't have the nerve to walk up to her to talk or introduce myself. About an hour after I had first spotted her, we found ourselves next to each other in the line for the bathroom. At that point, after drinking a fair amount of wine and smoking a couple of joints, I got the nerve to talk to her. The only comment I could come up with was, "You really look a lot like that girl in the bank commercial." Susan responded with, "Oh, you mean Sandy Duncan?" I replied, "Yeah, that's her!" and the ice had been broken. After both of us taking turns using the bathroom, I invited Susan outside to sit together and talk. We sat on the curb of the street and talked for what seemed like hours. She was so easy to talk to and we learned a lot about each other in a very short period of time. She wasn't planning on staying all night, so I think we were working on getting to know each other as quickly as we could. Suddenly, she realized the time was closing in on her curfew of midnight, and she started trying to remember what she had done with her dad's car. It suddenly came back to her, in the marijuana and alcohol—induced haze that she had loaned it to a couple of twin girls she knew, along with their common friend, a guy named Scott. They hadn't returned yet, and she was panicking about where the car was located. Another guy, Ray, who I think had an interest in Susan, volunteered to drive her around the neighborhoods and help her find it. Susan insisted that I go along, to Ray's apparent disappointment. After driving around for an hour or so, there had been no luck in locating the wayward car. Susan suggested that Ray drop her at her house and she would have to face the music in the morning when her dad awoke and found his car was missing. I convinced her to let Ray take us back to the apartment where the party was still going strong and see if they had returned. Lo and behold, when we arrived back at the all—night fest, there was the car parked in front of the apartment building. It turns out that the twins and Scott had driven to the beach and all dropped acid together. Susan quickly grabbed the keys from them and left for home at 12:45 a.m., well past her midnight curfew. Fortunately for her, when her mother heard her come in the front door and looked at the bedside clock, she misread the time as 11:55 p.m. instead of 12:55 a.m. In the morning, her mom commented how glad she was that Susan had returned just before her curfew, and had taken such good care of her father's car!

Susan and I fatefully met on June 4, 1971 at that crazy party and began cultivating our love relationship during what we both recall as the best summer of our lives. All of our free time was spent together, either at the beach during the day or with each other and friends at night. When we had been together for a couple of months, we started talking about our future together. We made daydream plans that we would get married right after high school, work full—time, and live in an apartment together. Who needed to worry about going on to college, adequate financial support, or having a family in the future? We were in love and living in the here and now.

The one difficult part of our relationship was when we talked about religion and the presence or absence of a greater power. Having been dutifully raised in the Catholic faith by my parents, I still had that inter-woven thread of faith in my life and wanted so badly to share it with Susan. Even though I had tried to ignore it during my teen years, that thread of faith was something that inexplicably bound me to the love of family, a knowledge that God existed, and the unforeseen future. The problem was that Susan had been raised with no religious upbringing and her life's spirituality came from sporadically attending the churches of friends and an interest in astrology and tarot cards that her paternal grandmother had relied on for daily guidance. When we would discuss the possibility of God, she would fervently say, "I don't know if there is a

God or heaven, and I'll find out when I die. I'm basically a good person. And if there is a God, He wouldn't condemn me for not knowing if He exists or not." The Catholic Church was also something that she didn't want to consider in her life. She had attended once or twice during her childhood with Catholic girlfriends and was very turned off by the doctrine and protocols of the church. This was one area of our relationship that was off limits for discussion, and my compromise was to put my faith in the back of my mind and overlook its absence. Despite the lack of a shared faith, we were continually growing in our love for one another. After high school graduation, we came to the practical realization that a real job in life was going to require a college education. We both started classes, she at Mesa Community College two blocks from her parents' house, and me at San Diego State University (SDSU). I had no idea what I was going to do in my life, but I did know that life sciences, especially biology, held the most interest for me. I had been part of a scuba diving group my last year and a half in high school and considered marine biology a possibility. I also threw in the forestry service for consideration. My mother had always wanted me to be a doctor and used to tell me as an infant, "Someday, you are going to be a doctor." I briefly considered pre—med studies, but it just seemed like such a long haul of between eleven and fifteen years of college, medical school, and residency training. It was just too hard for me to imagine the discipline that would be required to walk such a path.

During late high school and the college years at SDSU, I worked numerous part—time jobs. I have been everything from a maker of rabbit fur purses, to a sheet metal fabricator, to a woodworker laminating wooden strips into sheets of butcher block for tables and furniture. Susan's mother, Doris, worked at Mesa College and had a good friend who managed the job center for students. This made it very easy to find part—time jobs. Whenever I was out of work, she would pass the information for a new part—time job to Susan's mom before it had been added to the general bulletin board. I would end up being the first inquiring applicant and would usually get hired before any other students even knew about the job. It was pretty amazing when I think about all the diversity in my employment history thanks to this system. In the summer between my first and second years at SDSU, I was out of work and had Doris call her friend to see what was newly open.

There was a posting for "delivering door hangers" to advertise for a new start—up plumbing company. I applied and, because I had my own car, was hired immediately. The new company was located on Garnet Street in Pacific Beach and was opened by a couple who had run a very successful plumbing service company in Manhattan Beach near Los Angeles. They sold the company at its peak and moved to Zihuatenejo, Mexico. They lived there six months, saving enough of their money to begin the new start—up in San Diego. My role would be to saturate the neighborhoods of Pacific Beach, La Jolla, Mount Soledad, Mission Beach, and Clairemont with advertising placards for the new plumbing company by hanging them on the front door handles of the houses in these areas. I had no problem with this job, especially since the plumbing contractor and his wife were willing to pay me $3.00 per hour, nearly double the going minimum wage of $1.65. The part—time job involved me using my car to drive a team of teenagers and college students to perform the work along with me. Susan also was able to use the job pipeline to ensure she was always employed during her college years. She was able to obtain a union job working as the secretary for the union representative and was paid a very high hourly wage for those days. Both of us had plenty of money, were able to purchase new cars, and took the step of moving out of our parents' houses.

I had begun to work as a plumber's helper with the owner and the other plumbers in the company and quickly learned the terminology of fittings, grades of pipe, soldering copper water lines, and installing fixtures and water heaters. I continued to attend SDSU, but it was becoming apparent that my help was needed as a plumber as the company grew. The owner threw down the gauntlet that I had to decide between college and working as a plumber. It was an easy decision at that time, as I was making $7.00 per hour working as a plumber. This was more than triple the going minimum wage, and I enjoyed the hands—on work and learning to be a craftsman. I continued at SDSU with night classes working toward my bachelor's degree.

When Susan and I had moved out of the house, we each had our own apartments. She had been living on her own with roommates, her good friends Diana and Kathy, for about six months prior to my leaving home. In fact, when the three of them first moved out at the start of summer, they all lost their jobs in an untimely coincidence. Needing to pay one third of the rent and utilities, they all applied for unemployment and commodity foods. I had openings on the door hanger crew and was able to provide under—the—table income for them until the fall.

In October of that year, I moved into a furnished apartment about a mile from the place Susan shared with Diana at the time. Kathy had moved on to college at UC Irvine, so the two of them found a nice two—bedroom apartment. Susan spent the first night with me in my new apartment, but we made it clear to each other that this might be frowned on by both of our parents and it would only happen sporadically. Best intentions aside, she spent the second night, the third, and so on. After about four months of playing house, including hiding her clothes and makeup when my parents came over for dinner one night, we began to talk about getting married. This would be a big step in our lives; and, frankly, I wasn't completely sure it was the right thing to do. I had met a couple of other girls while at SDSU but never pursued relationships with them since I was attached to Susan. I didn't know if I was ready to make such a permanent commitment as marriage. I did know, however, that I loved Susan very much and I didn't want to lose her. I quickly buried the "grass is greener" perspective, and we set a wedding date. I think that very few young adults can say at the age of twenty that they are 100 percent sure they are ready for marriage.

Part of the impetus to get married was that Larry had hooked up with Susan's best friend since early junior high school, Gail. The two of them were married about one year prior to us. Larry was attending UCLA in pre—med studies, and they lived near campus in Westwood. We were attendants in the wedding, which was held in the chapel at the Naval Training Center in San Diego.

When I told my parents we were getting married, my mother questioned, "When you finish college?" I told her no, that we had set a date of April 19, 1975, which was about six months in the future. She pleaded with me to finish college, and I assured her I would by taking night classes. The promise was sincere, but I think mom knew it would be hard to do once married and making the wages we were being paid.

Susan and I began planning and negotiating the site of the wedding. Initially, she wanted to get married outside, overlooking the ocean, but this wasn't something allowed by the Catholic Church. She knew that even though I wasn't active in the church, I wanted a Catholic wedding. We decided on the compromise of a Catholic wedding without a full mass since it would lengthen the ceremony and the majority of the family and guests were not Catholic. Susan came up with the idea of being married at the San Diego De Alcala Mission. She envisioned the wedding party wearing Mexican peasant dresses and shirts, along with sandals, in the old mission church. We found out after researching the option that unless we were members of the parish, it would cost us a significant visitor's fee, a whopping fifty dollars, to use the mission. Since Susan's parents didn't have surplus money to cover the costs of the wedding, the two of us ended up paying for the majority of the expenses and the mission idea was dropped. We ended up with the next option: my parents' parish of Saint Mary Magdalene, a large church overlooking Mission Bay.

Our wedding was not the ideal dream that every young woman has as she marries her Prince Charming. The bridal gown and bridesmaids' dresses were all homemade, mostly by my mother. The men all wore polyester tuxedos, white jackets with black trim and black pants, and I was in a completely white tux. All of the men had long hair at or below their shoulders and a whole lot of facial hair. We fondly remember the event as the hairy polyester wedding. Since funds were limited, the reception was held in Susan's parents' backyard. Virtually all of the food was prepared by Susan's family, but we did spend the money to have a real three—tiered wedding cake. The most popular location in the backyard was around the keg of beer, with my plumber co—workers holding down the tap to serve the guests intermittently between their refills. Both Susan and I had illnesses leading up to our wedding, tonsillitis for her and bronchitis for me. Consequently, we both felt rotten the day of our wedding and couldn't fully enjoy ourselves or the food that had been prepared. The throwing of the bouquet and garter occurred from atop an ice plant covered embankment. Our wedding night was spent at a hotel on San Diego Bay, and we did have enough reserve to enjoy that part of the day. The best thing about it was thinking that all of our family and friends knew what we were doing and it was now okay.

Our honeymoon was a trip in my Ford Courier pickup and camper shell to Yosemite National Park, crossing to the coast for stops in Carmel, Hearst Castle, and down the Pacific back to San Diego. In Yosemite, we nearly froze overnight despite sleeping bags and awoke the next morning with fevers and feeling close to dead. We went to the small clinic in the valley, and all of the medical staff thought it was so funny that we were both sick on our honeymoon. After a couple of penicillin shots in the rumps, we headed for the warmer weather of the coast.

By the time we got into Carmel, all I wanted to do was lie in bed and suffer through it. Susan wanted to shop in all the beautiful stores, so she set out on her own. To this day, she remembers walking around alone and crying at the disappointment of our honeymoon.

Despite our whole wedding experience being somewhat of a disenchantment, we must have done something right. In April of 2010, we celebrated our thirty—fifth wedding anniversary with a family trip to the Bahamas!

After returning to San Diego at the end of the honeymoon trip, we moved to a rented condominium in Pacific Beach. Six months later, we bought our first home, a two—bedroom townhouse in Mira Mesa at the north edge of San Diego City. We did this to be able to have a dog and, immediately after moving, picked out our first baby at the Humane Society: Kimba, a fuzzy fur ball of a mutt.

We were living a very comfortable life between the two of us and the new member of our small family. We had sufficient money to enjoy short trips with friends and weekend dates. However, there was one critical part of our marriage that was missing: a shared faith in God. It was something we just never talked about; and I ignored the empty cup of spirituality, not wanting to push the issue with Susan. However, when God is working in your life, you can only ignore Him for so long, and things were about to dramatically change for us.

NEW LIFE DAWNS

Susan and I were twenty—three years old in 1977 and had been married for two years. We were living in a new house in the same area of Mira Mesa except larger with three bedrooms and two baths. We were beginning to talk about starting a family and decided this was as good as any time to begin trying. We actually dispensed with contraception in December of 1976; and by mid February 1977, we were blessed with the good news of a new family member on the way. It was stressful enough to be expecting a new baby after taking on a higher house payment. Then, about two to three weeks after we moved in, the manager of the plumbing company, another Mike, called and wanted to talk to me. I invited him to our house on a Sunday afternoon. He dropped by to inform me he was leaving the company and opening his own plumbing business. The shocker was that he wanted me to join him in a partnership. I quickly told him I had no extra money to invest, and said, "No problem. I've got five hundred dollars for initial materials and advertising, and we both have our own tools and pickup trucks." I told him I would have to talk it over with Susan and I would call him later.

In my youthful ignorance, I couldn't imagine that we wouldn't be successful. After long consideration, I got Susan's approval and her agreement to answer phones and handle accounting duties. She had spent the past two years managing the accounts receivable in a similar startup company that produced electronic controls for manufacturing companies, so she had extensive knowledge of basic business accounting.

I called Mike and told him I was in. I used up my saved vacation at the first plumbing company and then turned in my resignation. The owner and his wife were justifiably disappointed that I hadn't given them more notice and come to talk with them about the decision. They had taken me along from a clueless teenager to teaching me a trade I could rely on for my entire life. I didn't even have the courtesy to tell them in person I was leaving; I called them on the phone. I still regret to this day that I was so rude and gutless in the way I handled the situation.

The first day of February 1977 saw the birth of Reliable Plumbing, a two—man residential repair company. Our plan was to saturate neighborhoods with similar doorhangers that had started this whole journey off for me four years earlier. Our first job came within a day or two, and it consisted of installing a new water heater in a mobile home. Mike and I never had so much fun at work, especially when the owner wrote that first check for us to deposit in our business account.

So here Susan and I were, with no guaranteed income, a $325.00—per—month house payment, and a baby on the way. Sometimes in life, youthful exuberance overtakes practical common sense. But we were young and resilient and never doubted we could do it all. We survived the transition to self—employment, and the business grew enough to provide a fairly steady income of $250 per week for each of the two of us Mikes.

These were big changes for Susan and I, but the biggest was about to happen in October of 1977.

Susan had the largest abdomen I have ever seen on a woman in her ninth month of pregnancy. She wasn't fat, but it was obvious that our baby was going to be fairly big. Ultrasounds were not in common use yet for obstetric exams, so we had no idea of the sex of our baby. With my mom's assistance, we painted the nursery yellow and decorated in a gender—neutral theme of jungle wallpaper on one wall and animal print linens and blankets. We were ready in plenty of time for the due date of October 5.

Kathy, the same girl I was supposed to be hooked up with on that fateful party night, had met a co—worker in LA who fell in love with her at first sight. Chuck was an African—American who was raised in relative affluence. His father was an anesthesiologist with a very successful Los Angeles practice, and Chuck had attended Catholic schools most of his childhood. Kathy and Chuck were married a few months after meeting and about a year prior to us. They moved down to San Diego after spending a six—month—long sojourn in Europe, and we quickly came to like Chuck. They lived with us in my apartment for almost six months until our wedding day. It was tight space, with them sleeping on a fold—out couch, but we made it work. When we moved after our honeymoon, they also had to find an apartment and moved down to the beach, between Pacific Beach and Mission Beach. The four of us spent a lot of time together, as we were also living in the eastern end of Pacific Beach before our move to Mira Mesa. Kathy and Chuck threw a party for me on my twenty—first birthday at their apartment. Susan and I had just been married for three months, and the party was raucous and crowded for a one bedroom apartment. At one point, after I had a significant amount of alcohol, two cute young beach girls sat down to talk with me on the living room floor. Susan was in the kitchen and wasn't aware of them yet, but I was flattered to have two girls hitting on me. When Susan noticed what was going on, she immediately came up and asked me, "What are you doing?" I replied I was talking with the two girls, and promptly introduced Susan to them by saying, "This is my friend, Susan." Her face turned to a deep red with anger, and she loudly proclaimed, "Your friend!?, Hell I'm your wife!"

As Susan neared delivery of our baby, Kathy and Chuck spent a lot of time with us, anticipating the birth. One night a few days after her due date, she began having contractions, and Kathy and Chuck were at our house with us. The four of us sat for several hours and counted contractions, thinking this was it. It wasn't. In fact, we had several similar false starts as the baby became further delayed past the due date. Then, one night about fifteen days past the due date, I was sound asleep. Around 2:30 a.m. Susan got up to use the bathroom and yelled, "Wake up, Mike! My water just broke!" I was so fast asleep and groggily answered back, "Are you sure? I'm asleep!" It was pretty clear that she was right when she tersely shot back with, "I've got water pouring out from between my legs, and I'm not peeing!"

I jumped out of bed, grabbed our packed bag, and helped her to the car. Not knowing how long we'd be gone, I quickly fed our new cat, Rusty, who lived in the house, and our two dogs, Kimba and Hutch: Hutch was a lonely terrier we rescued after his owners, who worked with Susan, had died together in a car accident. The dogs lived outside in the garage and had access to our backyard, so I knew they would be fine for a while. The drive from our house to Sharp Memorial Hospital in Kearny Mesa was about fifteen miles, so I was flying down the freeway that was empty of traffic. Susan asked me to slow down since her contractions were just starting. She wisely told me that we could not be a family if we were all killed on the way to the hospital.

Labor was intensifying as we arrived at the hospital. We had done all the prenatal visits with Susan's family doctor, a general practitioner who had completed just an internship prior to starting private practice. He had been in Kearny Mesa for over twenty years and had cared for many of our friends and neighbors, so we had complete trust in him. Moreover, pregnancy and delivery of a baby was not covered by our health insurance, so we had made monthly payments to the doctor leading up to the birth. We certainly couldn't cover the cost of an OB—GYN for the care, so the family doctor was our only option. We had arrived at labor and delivery around 3:30 a.m., and I did my best to sleep in a recliner chair, with Susan having regular, intense contractions next to me. The days of Lamaze and the involvement of the father in the entire process had not yet become a standard practice. Susan got really irritated when the nurse came in to offer me a pillow and blanket. But the boiling point was reached around 7:00 a.m., when the nurse asked if I wanted some orange juice and donuts.

She was taken into the delivery room for the final part of labor, and I was offered the opportunity to gown and come into the room when the baby was coming out. I excitedly confirmed I wanted to be there.

So I got gowned and capped and waited anxiously in the labor room. Around 8:55 a.m., the nurse came to get me. I walked into the delivery room and must have had a horrified look on my face as I first took in the scene. The doctor was vigorously pulling on my baby's head with a pair of large metal forceps.

"He's in the military position and we're just helping him a little bit to come out."

Military position was face down with the chin extended upward, making it difficult for the head to navigate the birth canal. The doctor asked me to come over and pull on Susan's shoulders to keep her from being pulled down the delivery table. Assisting to keep her on the table, I really wondered what would happen if he pulled so hard the baby's head came off. Fortunately, after about a minute of pulling and manipulation, my baby boy was born, with head intact and crying loudly. Time of birth was 9:00 a.m. on Thursday, October 20, 1977, and he weighed in at eight pounds fourteen ounces. He was washed and swaddled in a blanket, and then Susan was allowed to hold him briefly, before they took him to the nursery for all the normal post—partum exams and eye medication. After Susan delivered the placenta and was cleaned up, we were taken to a side hallway. Our labor room had been occupied by a new patient, and discharges had not been completed yet to open up a post—partum room for us. One kind nurse did ask if we wanted our baby to hold while we waited for a room, and we jumped at the chance. She brought our new baby boy, whom we had decided would be named David Michael, from the nursery and laid him in Susan's arms on the gurney. He was so beautiful and peaceful as he slept in her arms.

She looked up at me with a tired appearance but wide smile on her face and said, "Look what we made. This is our baby, David!" I replied, "He's such a beautiful new life," as I thought to myself, I wish Susan could give the credit to God for this new infant, but I knew that wouldn't happen this day. Maybe someday it could happen.

We went home after three days in the hospital and began to assimilate our new roles as parents. David slept in his own room, the nursery, from the first night home. Because I was self—employed, there was no paternity time off, as we would lose income. I returned to work immediately, checking in with Susan once or twice a day when near a phone in the office or a payphone when out on jobs. Cell phones were just being invented in 1977 and were large, unwieldy contraptions that looked like a military field radio. They also were extremely expensive and had limited service areas. She also had the option of paging me if she had any problems I needed to help resolve.

On Wednesday, October 26, I routinely drove into our office to start the workday and was greeted by my partner, Mike, running frantically to my truck as I entered the driveway.

I rolled down the window, and he shouted at me, "Turn around and get home! Susan is hemorrhaging!"

Without even questioning what was going on, I sped out of the parking lot and back to the freeway to get home. I was driving as fast as I could, blinking my lights and honking my horn for slower cars to make way. I should have remembered Susan's earlier advice when she went into labor and realized that if I got killed en route, I wouldn't be able to help her at all. However, I was envisioning her lying on the floor at home, bleeding to death, and had to get there as quickly as I could. When I arrived home, she was sitting up and had just gotten off the phone with the doctor's office. The bleeding had slowed down, and he told her to have me bring her into the clinic. When we arrived, baby in hand, they roomed her right away and the family doctor examined her. The bleeding was minimal, and her vital signs were all stable. He prescribed some medication to help contract her uterus and sent us home.

When we returned home, everything seemed out of sorts. Susan started talking about a feeling she was having that she was going to die. I told her not to talk that way, but she kept describing a premonition of descending into a deep darkness. I said that she was probably having some post—partum hormone effects or mild depression and to try to focus on our new baby boy. I walked into the nursery to check on David and was completely abhorred when I saw several fleas on his forehead and body. Apparently, the cat had picked up fleas from outside; and with her shut in while we were at the hospital during the delivery, they had multiplied and spread throughout the house. On Thursday morning, we packed up the baby and supplies, I set off insecticide bombs, and we temporarily moved to Susan's parents' house to spend a couple of days.

Her bleeding seemed controlled at this point, but she persisted in talking about her premonition of impending death. I was worried, but didn't know how to assure her she was wrong.

That night, while at my in—laws,' Bill and Doris's house, Susan began to bleed uncontrollably. She was filling the toilet with large, bright—red clots of blood. I had never seen so much blood in my life. While her mother helped her, I called the emergency number for her family doctor. The operator connected me, and he said to drive her immediately to the emergency room at Sharp Hospital and he would meet us there. We arrived around four in the morning, and the doctor was arriving as we entered the ER.

I was beginning to feel so distraught, as though we had descended into some kind of hell over the past two days. "This isn't the way parenthood should begin!" I screamed inside. My baby was with my in—laws and my wife was bleeding profusely, all the while talking about impending death. She was even telling her family doctor about these feelings. He pulled me aside at one point and told me he was nervous and concerned about what she was saying. I asked him what we could do to stop the bleeding and convince her to stop saying she was going to die. He seemed at a loss for words.

Then, slowly, he said, "We'll get some IV fluids into her and I'll send off some lab tests to see how much blood she has lost. I'll also order some medication to help her uterus contract, and hopefully this will stop the bleeding."

I had never felt as helpless in my life as I did at that point, but it was going to get a lot worse before it got any better.

Around 6:30 a.m., I was beginning to feel we had been abandoned. Finally, the family doctor walked in to check on Susan. She was asking for a blood transfusion, as she began to feel weaker and weaker. Bright—red clots continued to accumulate on the bed shield underneath her. He agreed to order a couple of units of blood and went out to get it ordered. The ER nurse, whom we hadn't seen in close to an hour, shuffled into the room wrapped in her sweater and yawning.

"I'm almost off my night shift, but I want to get your vital signs for the oncoming nurse," she mumbled in between yawns.

Susan was beginning to look very pale and pleadingly looked at me.

"This is the feeling I knew was coming, Mike. I feel like I'm slipping away into a darkness I might not come back from. I think I'm dying."

With tears in my eyes, I told her not to think that and to hang on.

Suddenly, the tired, yawning nurse looked very anxious and worried. "I can't get her blood pressure," she stated out loud as Susan's eyes closed.

She ran out of the room and quickly ran back in with another doctor I had never seen. He was the OB—GYN on call to the ER and had been called in by the family doctor. He felt for a pulse and, not getting one, yelled to the nurse to call a code in the ER. He grabbed Susan's gurney and began wheeling her quickly into a resuscitation room.

At that point, as I followed the crowd gathering at the door to the resuscitation room, someone told me to wait back in the room we had been in and they would let me know how things were going when they were able. The overhead speaker blared over and over, "Code Blue, ER. Code Blue, ER." I was completely frantic, confused, and turned around. I walked to a door that exited into the waiting room and began pounding the wall next to it.

"Don't let her die! Please, God! Please!" I wailed to nobody in particular.

One of the clerks at the desk came up to me and told me my mother was in the waiting room and asked if I was aware she was there. I ran out the door and saw my mother as she asked me what was happening.

"It's bad, Mom. It's really bad. Susan might be dying," I cried as she cradled me in her arms.

Someone helped us back into the exam room where we had started the nightmare. I pulled myself together enough to tell my mom what was going on and that I had no idea if Susan was alive or dead. My mother had picked up Doris and my new son, David, before coming to the ER, so she left briefly to get the two of them from the car and bring them into the room. As I stood staring at my new baby boy through tear—filled eyes, I tried not to think about raising him alone, without his mother, but the thought wouldn't leave my mind. Someone had called a priest who arrived a few minutes later. He was an older clergyman who was assigned in the waning years of his vocation as a chaplain for the hospital. It was obvious he was very nervous in such tense situations, as he began trying to ease us with lighthearted jokes, some of which, quite frankly, I found distasteful. I tried to redirect him to the reason he was there but, in my confusion, asked if we should baptize my baby. Perplexed, he asked if something was wrong with the infant. My mom explained that I was very stressed and dazed by the past hours and that it was my wife who was critically ill.

We all remained uncomfortably crowded in the little room for what must have been close to forty—five minutes. Finally, someone came to get me.

"She's awake, and you can see her for just a few minutes before they take her to the operating room," I was told by the staff person.

I rushed into the resuscitation room and straight to Susan's side. Multiple IVs were in her arms, two with blood being delivered.

She had a wild—eyed look to her as she gushed out to me, "That was it. That was the feeling I've been having for the past week. I felt like I was going to die. And I did, but they brought me back. I must have ESP to know that was going to happen."

She kept impressing upon me that it was through clairvoyance or ESP that all of the prior events had been predicted by her. I let her believe that idea, but I was beginning to feel that a higher hand was involved in getting us through the hellish maze of the past week.

The OB—GYN doctor wanted to get her quickly to the OR, so he rapidly explained to me that he was taking her for a dilatation and curettage to try to stop the continuing bleeding. However, if that didn't stop the hemorrhage, he would need to perform an emergency hysterectomy to stabilize her. I looked at Susan and told her we could always adopt to have more children, but I wasn't going to lose her at any cost. They wheeled her away after I kissed her forehead and told her I would see her when she got out of the surgery.

GOD WORKS IN MYSTERIOUS WAYS

When Susan was taken to the recovery room, the OB—GYN doctor found me and gave me the wonderful news that all bleeding had been stopped with the D&C and there was no need for a hysterectomy. She was going to need to stay in the hospital for a few days but could breastfeed David in her room. Her good friend and co—worker in the accounting office, Vicki, came to see both her and David and also brought the good news that all of the post—partum hospital expenses were covered by Susan's company group health insurance. That was the last worry on my mind, as I was just so grateful to have my wife and the mother of my new, beautiful son alive and recovering. Susan was compelled to share with Vicki her premonition of impending death and credited ESP or a sixth sense for her awareness of all of the events that occurred . Vicki was not a particularly religious person and was intrigued by it all, concurring with Susan that it must ESP.

During this second hospitalization, I stayed at my parents' house with David starting on Friday, the day of her near—death. We visited Susan all day long on Saturday and then returned Saturday night to my parent's place. I was feeling completely exhausted by this whole ordeal and passed out in bed around 9:00 p.m. on Saturday night. My mother was able to feed David with bottles and volunteered to get up throughout the night as needed. Her love and devotion to me and my son were irreplaceable during this difficult time.

I woke to a start as my bedroom door was opened at 6:00 a.m. It was my dad, and he said Susan was on the phone and had to talk to me immediately. He also told me it sounded like she was crying. My heart started pounding as I considered the possibilities. Was she bleeding again? Were they taking her back to the OR for a hysterectomy? What could be so important to call me at such an early time on a Sunday morning?

I got to the phone and picked it up, asking what was wrong. Susan told me there was nothing wrong but she needed very badly to see me immediately. Then, after a pause, she said, "Mike, I need to go to church this morning."

I was completely floored. Where had this come from? We hadn't talked about religion, faith, or God in several years, and it was never something I would expect from Susan.

I asked what had caused this sudden need to go to church; and she replied, "It's incredibly complicated, and I'll tell you about it when you get here."

I told her I would get dressed quickly and be right over to the hospital. After getting ready to leave, I briefly told my parents the reason for my hasty departure and asked if they could care for David for a couple of hours. They were happy to do so, and right as I was ready to leave, I asked them if they could loan me a Bible.

I hadn't opened a Bible in many years and really didn't know how exactly I was going to explain to Susan the roots of my faith. And more importantly, how was I going to talk to her about Jesus and what he meant to that faith?

As I arrived at the hospital, I realized it was presumptuous of me to assume she wanted to go to my church, so I decided I would start slowly and explore what she wanted and needed.

I came into her room, and while it looked like she had been crying at some point, there was a glow of happiness surrounding her. "So what brought all of this about?" I questioned.

"Let's go outside and sit on the bench," she suggested.

It was a beautiful Sunday morning, the sun warming the grounds outside her room, and we sat on a bench together just on the edge of some grass.

She began slowly, "Early this morning, I was lying awake in my bed and trying to come to some understanding of why I almost died and how I came to know it was going to happen days before it actually occurred. I definitely wasn't asleep, and I know this was no dream. Suddenly, I felt the presence of a higher being filling my room and completely enveloping me. I then felt my soul rise above my body. It was similar to how I felt as I was bleeding to death but much more peaceful and calming. In fact, it felt so incredible to be free of an earthly body that part of me didn't want to go back, but I knew I had a new baby and didn't want to leave you alone to raise him. I didn't see anything and didn't hear His voice. But somehow, He communicated with me. The knowledge was imparted into me, *"I give life and I can take life away."* I felt as though I was in a court of law, pleading to continue living and being able to raise my new baby boy. I also sensed that there were other people or souls surrounding me. Then, just as suddenly, I was back in my body and knew right away that I had to get to church as soon as possible."

Knowing the concerns Susan had expressed in the past about the Catholic Church, I told her that we didn't have to be Catholics. We could attend any church she wanted, and I would make it work.

"No," she said. "We have to join the Catholic Church."

When I asked why, she responded that it had been my faith that had saved her life and she wanted to know everything she could about that faith. I told her that they wouldn't let her leave to go to church but showed her the Bible and suggested that we look at it together. I opened the Bible to the New Testament, and there, holding the place, was a prayer card with a beautiful painting of the Living Christ. For hours, it seemed, we talked about Jesus and His being the absolute foundation of the Catholic faith. She remembered stories and parables she had heard while attending Sunday school with friends and asked me about everything I knew regarding them. It was the most incredible morning, and I didn't want it to ever end.

I left the Bible with her to read, if she could, between feeding David and recovering herself.

When I left that afternoon, I was still in complete awe that such an incredible conversion could occur for my wife. Susan was and is a very rational and objective person, and I knew that what she was telling me had to have really occurred. I spent the next several days in complete awe of God's power as I shared the story with family, friends, and anyone I could tell about it. To this very day, Susan has no fear of dying and deeply knows that there is a beautiful eternity that awaits us on the other side of the transition. Dying is just the beginning.

Susan wasn't going to be discharged for another couple of days, and Monday was the first post—partum well—baby checkup for David. Kathy and Chuck were with Susan in her room, listening as she recounted the incredible events of the past three days. When I arrived with baby David, they were so taken with how cute and peaceful he looked when they first saw him. I invited Chuck to help me take him to the doctor's office, so we set off to the car. When we arrived at the clinic office, we got a lot of stares from the other adult patients. Then I realized that they all must have been wondering what a skinny, long—haired surf bum and a black man with a huge Afro hairdo were doing with a newborn baby. You just never know what you're going to see in life at any time or place.

BUILDING A SHARED FAITH

When life settled down and we started to get used to being parents, we decided it would be easiest to start going to Mass with my parents at St. Mary Magdalene. We knew that eventually, we would need to locate and join the parish in our neighborhood, as the drive to St. Mary Magdalene was some twenty—five to thirty minutes each way. We decided we would make the change after David was baptized. There was one priest in particular whom we really liked at St. Mary Magdalene, a younger, energetic man named Father Rusty. His spirituality shone all around him, and he was extremely intelligent. We had decided we wanted Kathy and Chuck to be David's Godparents. I set up an appointment on a Sunday evening to meet with Fr. Rusty to discuss the baptism and to clarify some questions we had about it. For one, Kathy was Methodist, not Catholic, and we wanted reassurance that wouldn't be an issue. The four of us met at my parent's house, and we all drove to the church together. We knocked on the door of the rectory, and Fr. Rusty opened it. Hanging around his neck was a simple but elegant wooden cross on a leather string.

Noticing that all four of us were gazing at it, Fr. Rusty invited us in as he said, "I'm not a Jesus freak or anything. I've just been on a retreat all weekend, and this cross was a gift during it."

With that, we all relaxed and got to know Fr. Rusty much better over the next couple of hours. Kathy was perfectly fine to be the Godmother, as long as she was a baptized Christian. Chuck, of course, had been raised very Catholic, although he was currently not practicing his faith. Hopefully, David's baptism might be the spark that could rekindle his spirituality. During the baptism the next Saturday, we all got a good laugh when David began sucking on Father Rusty's thumb as he was signing him on the lips.

After David was baptized, we kept to our plan and began attending the Catholic Church in Mira Mesa, Good Shepherd Parish. One Sunday, after mass, we stopped into the local McDonald's for breakfast. A young man dressed in black slacks, a black shirt, and a brightly colored tee shirt under it stopped at our table to admire David. He had wild, unruly, blonde hair and an outgoing personality. After he left, we both wondered if he was a minister or priest from the area, as we had never seen him before. Neither of us had the courage to go and ask him, so we finished our breakfast and left.

Within a week or two, Susan inquired in the rectory office about our joining the parish and her starting some type of class or training to join the church and receive the sacraments. There had been four other young women who were waiting for a group to start, all led by Deacon Dan, a transitional deacon. He was a seminarian who had been ordained as a deacon in transition to becoming a fully ordained priest. Susan added her name to attend the first gathering of all of them a few days after her inquiry. When she walked into a conference room, there, waiting for everyone to arrive, was the wild—haired young man we had briefly met in McDonald's.

Deacon Dan was overflowing with spirituality and a love for playing the guitar. Every week, this group of young women would meet together with Dan for six hours or so of learning about the Catholic faith and life in general. They took field trips to other churches, read Scripture, sang songs, and learned to pray together. This was the early stage of a new process that was resurrected in the Catholic Church by Vatican II called the Rite of Christian Initiation for Adults or RCIA. They were going through the process that would, as an in—depth journey of conversion, ultimately led to Confirmation, the Sacrament that represents full embodiment of the Catholic faith.

The five women shared so much together. They developed a deep and personal friendship that would last a lifetime. Susan and Carol, a young woman three years older than Susan, became especially close and supportive of one another. Carol had a new baby girl, Mandy, the same age as David, as well as a three—year—old boy, Bobby. Her husband, Bob, had been raised Catholic in a very Italian family, and Carol decided it was time for her to join the Catholic faith and raise her children in that same loving faith. She and Susan spent a lot of time together both in the group and on their own. Over the years, Carol babysat David as Susan went back to work part—time to help supplement our income. Bob and I also became close and started playing racquetball together one night a week. Both of our families went camping in the desert together, swam in their backyard pool, and eventually helped support a church youth group together. We put on Catholic weekend retreats for high school and early college students called Daybreak. This consisted of various team members sharing spiritual stories and events in their lives. Susan and I always seemed to be asked to handle the marriage talk. When we recounted our early years together and Susan's incredible story of near—death and conversion, there was never a dry eye in the group. Working on these retreats also grounded us in our faith and certainly made the day—to—day grind of work and running a business shrink to a much lower priority for a while.

We developed a deep and important relationship with our friends and fellow Christians at Good Shepherd Parish and attended a marriage encounter weekend retreat. This was a retreat for married couples to deepen their relationship and learn to better communicate with one another. After the retreat, we got involved in the marriage encounter community within the church, but we decided it wasn't right for us. It seemed as though the members tended to worship marriage encounter and what it represented more than God.

I was happy working as a plumbing contractor and especially enjoyed the hands—on aspect of the job. However, it seemed like I was squandering my interest in life sciences and wasn't doing something that was completely using my abilities.

I decided that going back to night school might be a solution for this feeling of inadequacy in my life. Bob and I both signed up for an Introduction to Business class at the community college. We stuck it out for about two months and then both decided it wasn't doing anything for us. We both had more practical business knowledge than anything they were teaching in the class.

I did, however, find that reading and studying seemed to wake up my brain and stimulate me to expand my horizons. The following semester, I took an astronomy course that revealed to me the expansiveness of the universe and the incredible energy it took to keep the complexity of planets, solar systems, and galaxies organized. One day, in the newspaper, I found an ad from an amateur astronomer who was selling a homemade, six—inch reflecting telescope. He fabricated his own scopes and had hand—ground the mirror for the one he was selling for the fifty—dollar asking price. I had my first stargazing telescope, and it opened the heavens to my human eye in a way never seen before. It almost seemed like looking directly into God's creation as I explored the planets, moon, and star clusters. My love for astronomy has lasted my entire life, and with my current eleven—inch reflector telescope, viewing distant galaxies is a most spiritual experience. It was incredible to try to comprehend the concept that light from any of a number of galaxies that entered my eye through a telescope was emitted millions of years ago and was just reaching earth as I viewed it. This was and is an awe—inspiring realization of how expansive God's universe is and how we are but a tiny part of it.

One of my most favorite classes I ever attended during my return to school was an Introduction to Logic class at the community college. The instructor was an older man who exuded wisdom and was able to break philosophical complexities into understandable ideas. My favorite part of the course was how he logically explained, using the basic teleological arguments proposed by such Greek philosophers as Plato and Aristotle, the existence of a Superior Creator of the universe. The philosophers recognized evidence of an order or design to all matter in the universe. From the microcosms of earth to the organized human body to the heavens above, they were aware of some logical order to everything. Even though thermodynamics and the study's second law, the law of entropy, to our knowledge, had not yet been discovered, they knew there had to be some type of energy keeping this order intact. And if the energy wasn't present, all design and organization of matter would lapse into chaos.

The laws of thermodynamics are essential basic foundations of the studies of physics and chemistry. The second of the laws, or the law of entropy, states that without some ongoing input of energy, matter will gain entropy or disorganization and devolve into a chaotic mess. A simple example of entropy is the melting of ice. This energy that the ancient Greeks knew had to exist, they also reasoned, had to come from a Supreme Creator or Source.

As I took these classes, I felt as though I had awakened my brain for the first time in several years. I also began to study on my own what the precepts of my Catholic faith taught in regard to science and evolution. I had developed a scientifically inquisitive mind, and I just couldn't take the first book of the Bible, Genesis, as a literal description of the creation of the universe. This was especially true given all of the evidence being discovered in support of a progressive evolution of the universe and life on earth. Investigating books written by Catholic philosophers, theologians, and other authors besides the Bible, I learned that my own Catholic faith meshed perfectly with my scientific beliefs. The story in creation was seen as what it was, an allegory developed by a simple Hebrew race to explain how they and the world around them came to exist. My faith that I had been raised in did not deny the likelihood that God had created the universe and earth through an extremely complex plan of evolution and that comprehending how it all fit together was beyond our own simple understandings of nature and the universe. When I was coming to this realization that science and faith were inexplicably intertwined beyond our wildest dreams, the science of DNA was just beginning to be revealed and the concept of mapping the human genome had not even been proposed. Looking back on my own spiritual evolution, I believe that our human science is leading us on an infinite path toward God, Whom we can never fully reach in a lifetime.

While my faith and spiritual beliefs were expanding before me, so too were Susan's. She kept strong contacts with her women's group and, together, they supported Father Dan as he became a priest. Susan and Carol grew strong in their friendship and loved one another as though they were sisters. They became more and more involved in ministries at the church and, together, they became the co—leaders of the teenage girls' youth group.

I felt that Susan knew so much more than I did about the Catholic faith, even though it had just been a couple of years since her conversion. Our faith in God was blossoming in ways I never dreamed it could or would. Little did we know that in a year or so, our faith would be tested like never before.

TINY ANGEL, TINY CHRIST

We were elated when we found out Susan was pregnant again. David was just over two years old, and we felt that it was the right time for our family to grow. We had just moved into a larger two—story house in the Rancho Penasquitos development just north of the Mira Mesa area. It was about five minutes farther up the freeway when there was no traffic and gave us room in the house that we didn't have in the former home.

Our new baby was due October 5 in 1980, and we had prepared the nursery with many of David's hand—me—downs, such as the crib, dresser, and rocking chair. David was excited to be expecting a new little brother or sister. We were all hoping for a girl, David included, but we just wanted a happy, normal baby. We had tentatively selected Zachariah as the name if it was a boy and Jennifer as the name for a girl. Throughout that summer, we spent a lot of time around our in ground spa I had installed in our backyard, and Susan's abdomen never looked as large as it had with David. We were hoping that the baby was smaller because it was a girl.

As the end of summer approached, the plumbing business was starting to drop off from extremely successful years in 1978 and 1979. My partner Mike and I had bought an existing company that had been around for over twenty years and had seen the business grow from five service trucks to over thirty trucks and plumbers. The stress level was very high, as we often had to fight with customers to pay their bills on time and also had to deal with employee theft of materials, tools, and customers, as some plumbers would set up side jobs and take the money directly rather than running the job through the company. Mike and I at times felt like we had a revolving door of plumbers, and we came to realize that there was better loyalty if we hired inexperienced but hardworking men and trained them in the skill. Looking back on those years, we taught and trained some ten to twelve honest young men who, to this day, are running their own businesses around San Diego. In retrospect, that is a legacy I can take pride in, but it was difficult to see when I was twenty—five and in the heat of the battle.

On September 30 of that year, I was coming home in the mid afternoon a little earlier than usual in order to do some yard work and clean up. As I approached the corner to turn into my neighborhood, there, coming in the opposite direction, was Carol's truck. Susan was sitting in the passenger seat. Carol flagged me down with a frantic wave, and I pulled a u—turn at the corner and parked behind her. I ran to the driver's window, and Carol yelled to me that Susan's water had just broken. Unable to reach me while I was on the road home, Susan called Carol, who raced to our house to take her to the hospital. How could this be? It was nearly a week early, and we were expecting her to run late as she had with David. Oh well. It was time to have a new baby.

Carol also had David in the truck, so she was going to take him home with her while I continued the drive to the hospital. Susan got into my truck, and we set off for the Kaiser Permanente hospital, which was about fifteen miles south of Rancho Penasquitos in the Murphy Canyon area of Mission Valley. I knew it would be quite a long drive, given the time of day and the growing traffic volume in our home town, but I was much calmer and relaxed than the first time around with David.

Our close friend Kathy had applied to and been accepted into nursing school at San Diego State University's school of nursing. She was currently in her OB—GYN rotation and was following Susan in the pregnancy as her semester project. Susan and I had agreed to allow Kathy into the delivery with us, and I quickly asked if Susan had called her. During the unexpected event of her water breaking, she did have the presence of mind to let Kathy know we were on the way to Kaiser and would meet her in the labor and delivery area.

When we arrived at the hospital, Susan was having regular contractions and had started to dilate her cervix when examined by the labor and delivery nurse. Ultrasound was still not a routine modality in pregnancy but was starting to evolve in its use. A doctor came in pushing a portable machine and introduced himself. He told us he wanted to do a quick ultrasound to check the baby's position and measure the head circumference. When he placed the transducer on Susan's abdomen, the scan revealed that the baby was in a footling breach position, with one foot down into the birth canal. This position would not allow for a vaginal delivery, so we were consented for a Caesarian section to deliver the baby. By then, it was after 5:00 p.m., and we were placed into the hallway of the triage area to await the opening of an available operating room. This was and still is the only Kaiser Permanente hospital in the San Diego region; consequently, the hospital is extremely busy and crowded all the time.

While we waited for the OR, the anesthesiologist placed an epidural catheter and began medicating Susan to ease the pain of the contractions. Finally, a room was being turned over and cleaned to get ready for us. Kathy and I were given our gowns, hair and shoe covers, and masks to prepare to enter the room with Susan. When they took her in, we excitedly followed behind the gurney and received the instructions of where we were to stand. We were placed on either side of Susan's head, allowing enough room for the anesthesiologist to monitor her vitals and insure that her level of anesthesia was adequate to remove all sensation below her diaphragm. As the OB—GYN doctor cut into her lower abdomen, Kathy and I were very intrigued and making comments about her abdominal wall, the size and color of her uterus, and anything else that caught our attention. This mildly irritated Susan, since she was unable to see what we were looking at and commenting about. The doctor incised the uterus and deftly pulled out a very tiny baby girl. She was extremely blue and didn't cry immediately. The neonatal team dried her and took her right away to the nursery. We were told they were going to examine her and would bring her to us as soon as they were able. They were able to weigh her before they took her away, and she was quite little, weighing in at four pounds fifteen ounces. She was, however, about three weeks early by her size according to the doctor, even though she had been born just five days earlier than the due date. The doctor thought the original due date estimate might have been off and should have been later in October.

After Susan's incisions were closed, they rolled us into a post—partum recovery room.

After twenty minutes or so, a woman pediatrician came into our room and said, "The baby is breathing well and crying a little, but we've found an unexpected problem. She has a heart murmur, and we don't know yet what the problem is exactly."

I had known several kids during my school years that had heart murmurs, and I reassured Susan that it was common and usually no big deal. Kathy and I sat next to Susan in the post—partum room for almost an hour until a nurse came and took me to see our daughter. I walked into the newborn nursery, and there was our tiny angel under an oxygen hood but still with a bluish tinge. This was especially true of her lips and hands, although nothing as bad as she had looked during the delivery. She had an IV in the umbilical vein and was sleeping after the rude manner in which she was separated from the womb. A doctor came into the nursery and asked one of the staff if that was Dad standing near the baby.

"Does he know?" he questioned.

"Not yet," replied the nurse.

The doctor came over, introduced himself, and explained that he was the pediatric cardiologist on call. "Your baby girl has what is known as a cyanotic congenital heart defect. What defect we're not completely sure yet, but I'm expecting it is most likely tetralogy of fallot. This is where there are four classic abnormalities with the heart, including a ventricular septal defect, or VSD. This is a large hole between the two lower chambers, or ventricles. She is cyanotic, or bluish colored, because unoxygenated blood is crossing between the two lower chambers through this VSD and mixing with the blood flowing out to the body. She will most likely need surgery in the next day or so to temporarily shunt more blood to the lungs. This is needed to provide more oxygen to the body and vital organs. She needs to be transferred to either Children's Hospital or the University of California, San Diego Medical Center. It will most likely be UCSD, as the pediatric cardiothoracic surgeon for Children's is on vacation and is unlikely to return in the next twenty—four to forty—eight hours. I'm setting up the critical care transport team to pick up your baby and take her to the med center as soon as possible. You won't be able to ride in the ambulance but can follow them and see her as soon as they have her settled in the neonatal ICU."

My head was spinning at this incredulous news, and all I could say was, "Let's do whatever we have to do to get her help." I didn't know how I was going to break this news to Susan after what she had just been through with the C—section. I thanked the doctor and walked to her room. She and Kathy were on the edge, waiting to know anything about what was going on with our baby. I did my best to explain what they thought was wrong with her tiny heart and broke the news she would be going into surgery as soon as they could diagnose her exact defect. As I held Susan's hand, the transport team rolled our baby girl into the room in an incubator. They opened the cabinet, and with tears in her eyes, Susan stroked her tiny little hand and fingers. The team gave me directions to UCSD Medical Center from Kaiser, and Kathy offered to drive me there so I wouldn't have to worry about finding parking.

Prior to leaving for the med center, I had called Carol and Bob, as well as both sets of our parents, to tell them what news we knew. Bob and my parents all said they would meet me at UCSD. By then, it was around 11:00 p.m., and I told them they didn't have to come to the hospital, but the three insisted they wanted to be there. Carol would stay at home, watching over David and her children. The support of friends and family was invaluable as I tried to understand the rough path my wife, son, and I were about to walk.

Kathy drove up to the main entrance of the medical center to drop me off. Feeling helpless, she said she needed to do something for us but didn't know how she could help.

I told her, as she gave me a hug, "Just say lots of prayers for my baby girl and help Susan as much as you can in the next couple of days. She's not going to be able to come to the medical center for a few days, and it's going to be very hard on her sitting at Kaiser, knowing her new baby is being taken to surgery."

I entered through the front door and asked a security guard where the neonatal ICU was located. I was told it was on the second floor, so I grabbed the closest elevator and pushed the button for the second floor. When the doors opened, the critical care transport team was just arriving with my little angel. An ICU nurse pointed to a family waiting room and asked me to stay there until they got her settled in the ICU. Within a few minutes, Bob and my parents arrived as they had promised. I was just catching the three of them up on everything that I knew and had been told to expect when an Asian doctor in scrubs entered the family room. He introduced himself as the pediatric cardiology fellow and explained that his attending staff doctor was on his way into the hospital. The fellow explained to us that they were going to take my baby girl into a specialized operating room to perform a cardiac catheterization on her. This would provide moving images of her heart demonstrating the flow of blood and give them an exact diagnosis of what the congenital cardiac defect was and what needed to be done to repair it. He had me consent for the procedure and then went to await his attending to arrive and perform the procedure. An hour or so later, when they had completed the catheterization, the fellow and attending took the four of us into a conference room. The attending cardiologist began to draw on a chalk board how the abnormal flow of blood was occurring through my daughter's heart. My experience as a plumbing contractor helped me greatly in understanding everything he was telling me. I had significant experience in the installation of pumps and waterlines, which, in essence, was what he was talking about and drawing on the board. My baby girl did, indeed, have tetralogy of fallot (TOF). This is a common congenital cardiac abnormality in which there is a VSD, or hole, between the two pumping chambers of the heart, the ventricles. Both oxygenated and unoxygenated blood can move from one side to the other through this defect in the septum, or wall, between the two major chambers of the heart. In classic TOF, as the two doctors referred to it, the pulmonary artery that allows blood to flow into the lungs is narrowed and the aorta overrides the septum, or wall, between the two ventricles. In my baby's case, she had pulmonary atresia, or no main pulmonary artery whatsoever. She was alive only because a tiny connection between the aorta and the base of the left pulmonary artery was still open. This tiny connection is called the ductus arteriosus and is present to bypass the lungs while the baby is in the uterus and receiving oxygen through the umbilical cord. Once a normal baby is born, the lungs inflate and blood flows into them and circulates normally. The ductus normally closes within a couple of days to a week after birth. In my daughter's case, there was no blood flowing from the right ventricle of the heart into the main pulmonary artery, which was missing. The ductus allowed blood from the aorta to flow backward into the left and right pulmonary arteries into the lungs, providing some oxygenation of the blood. To keep her alive, she would need two interventions. The first was to make sure the ductus didn't close before they could operate on her and form a temporary bypass to feed blood into her lungs. In 1980, it was known that hormonelike substances called prostaglandins were instrumental in many biological functions within the human body. One of these substances, prostaglandins E1 or PGE1 as they referred to it was known to keep the ductus open longer than normal. They asked for and received my consent to administer this substance to my daughter. At the time, it was experimental and in clinical trials. Presently, it is in standard use for ductus—dependent congenital heart defects.

The second major intervention was to perform surgery to provide a bypass shunt to feed blood to the lungs while she grew larger and a permanent repair could be done. The surgery was called a Blalock—Taussig shunt, named after the surgeon and cardiologist who developed it at Johns Hopkins. In actuality, the procedure was developed and extensively tested on dogs by Blalock's laboratory assistant, Vivien Thomas. Thomas was African—American and in the mid 1940s, due to racial prejudice, Thomas was not accepted as a co—developer of the procedure by the faculty and medical community. He had no degree beyond a high school diploma but had the brilliance to refine this experimental procedure, and he even built the instruments used to perform it. In fact, he coached Blalock through the first one hundred operations on infants with TOF. A painting of Vivien Thomas hangs, to this day, in Johns Hopkins between that of Alfred Blalock and Helen Taussig.

The surgery would be scheduled for my daughter in twenty—four hours on the Thursday after her Tuesday—evening birth. In a B—T shunt, as it is referred to in the medical community, one of the subclavian arteries that feeds blood to the arms would be diverted and tied into the pulmonary artery to feed blood into the lungs instead. The arm would still receive blood flow, although diminished, from a network of arteries under the shoulder blade, or scapula, which flows into the main brachial artery of the affected arm.

After the two cardiologists had explained all of this information very clearly, the attending doctor wanted to impress upon me how this surgery would be the first of many if my daughter survived it and the beginning of a long, hard road. He then told me that if I didn't think my wife and I could handle such an emotional and stressful journey, we didn't have to consent to have the surgery done. They could make my daughter comfortable and allow nature to take its course.

Allowing nature to take its course meant that she would live for a few days until the ductus arteriosus closed and then she would die from lack of any oxygen in her blood.

I looked him square in the eyes and replied, "This is my baby daughter, and we need to do everything we can to give her a chance at life."

On Thursday morning, Susan was still in the hospital, recovering from the C—section. Carol and two other friends from her Catholic conversion class, Peggy and Vicki, arrived at 8:00 a.m. to be with her while our daughter was in surgery. I arrived at UCSD around 7:00 a.m. to wait with my baby girl in the NICU. The plan was to take her to the OR around 7:30 a.m., and I wanted to be there when she was taken. Just before the planned time, the pediatric cardiology fellow came into the NICU and delivered the disappointing news that a baby who was much more ill had come in the prior night and the surgeon had to bump my daughter to operate on the sicker infant. We would be rescheduled for Friday morning, and they would continue to administer the PGE1 to keep the ductus from closing.

I thought about calling Susan but decided I would just drive to Kaiser and tell her in person. When I came through the door into her room, all four women looked at me with horrified expressions, and Susan tensely questioned, "Why are you here?! What went wrong?" I immediately realized that they must be thinking that our baby girl had died, so I quickly reassured everyone that she was okay but her surgery had been postponed. Deflated—but—relieved sighs went through the room, and Susan asked me when they would operate. I told her we were definitely on for Friday morning since the longer we waited the greater the chance her ductus would close.

I spent several hours with my wife, and during the time I was with her, the staff person who prepared the birth certificates came in to have us complete the form. We had been planning on naming the baby Jennifer prior to her birth, but both of us felt that Jennifer didn't adequately reflect how blessed by God she was to even be alive. I don't remember who suggested it first, but Christina Marie was the name we both agreed she should be given. "Tiny Christ" fit perfectly, and thus our daughter was officially named.

I went back by the NICU at UCSD to see Christina before I began the drive north to pick up David for the night and get some rest before Friday morning. He was having such a great time at Carol and Bob's with their two kids, Bobby and Mandy, that Carol suggested I let him spend another night. She would take him to preschool in the morning and then return again to Susan's side to support her during the surgery. This sounded good to me, so I could get as much sleep as possible to be ready for the next round.

Sleep was difficult at best. I must have called the NICU four times throughout the night to check that Christina was still alive. I just couldn't relax enough to rely on the nurse taking care of her to let me know if there were any problems. After a few hours of exhausted sleep, I got up, showered, and drove down to the med center to be there by 7:00 a.m. again. This time, they took her to the OR and I went to wait in the main lobby where the surgeon told me he would come to find me after the surgery. My parents, in—laws, Kathy, and Bob all showed up shortly after I sat down, and we all waited nervously for several hours. My parents wanted me to go to the cafeteria for some breakfast, but I was far too anxiety—filled to eat anything. All I could do was sit, walk around, and pray to myself for God to keep her safe.

After about three hours, the cardiothoracic surgeon came out to find me. I was told that everything went as planned and that she was doing well in recovery. Her cyanosis was much improved but still partially present. The B—T shunt was only 2 millimeters in diameter and would most likely have to be revised in a year or so. That was okay with me, as my daughter was alive and given the chance to grow from an infant to at least a toddler. "Praise God," I kept saying as I hugged all of my supporters. I raced to a public phone down the hallway and called Susan in her hospital room this time around rather than scaring her as I did during the false start. She burst into tears of joy when she heard our baby was alive and doing well.

"I need to see her tomorrow, if they'll let me," she stated.

I told her we would see what her doctors thought.

That night, Carol and Bob brought David to Kaiser to see his mom. The last time he had seen Susan was Tuesday afternoon. After a couple of hours of intermittent visiting and playing with a wheelchair, my son and I drove home. We slept much better that night, ready for whatever the next day brought us. On Saturday, Susan was doing better, and her doctors decided to discharge her after only three full days of post—partum recovery, mainly so she could visit Christina at UCDMC. We drove over to the med center, and Susan slowly shuffled her way from the parking structure to the inside elevators. Holding her lower abdomen, she made her way with me as I took her to the NICU. David couldn't go into the unit, but there were glass windows where he could see his new baby sister in her incubator. Susan went in first and washed her hands and put a gown over her clothes. The nurse helped her take Christina in her arms and, looking past all the IV tubes and medication bags, mother and daughter fell in love.

Christina was in the NICU for seven days total, and then we finally got to bring her home to her new bedroom. It was so frightening to think of all the things that might go wrong with her in our care, that we were overwhelmed by the myriad of possibilities. Worry would only give us an ulcer and would not change what was to be, so we just decided to let go and let God. She slept in her crib from the very first night, and Susan got up only to breastfeed her in the early morning hours. Christy, as we started to call her, slowly started to gain weight. Starting from her birth weight of 4 pounds, 15 ounces, it took a while to even get to eight pounds. She developed normally and became quite an active infant and baby over the months.

Shortly after we had moved into our house in Rancho Penasquitos, we learned that a new priest was coming to our parish of Good Shepherd in Mira Mesa, where we had continued to be members. The new priest was transferring from Saint Mary Magdalene parish, where we were married, and was named Father Rusty. We couldn't believe that he was joining our parish family! We wanted Christy baptized as soon as possible, even though a Catholic nurse in the NICU had done an emergency baptism before her surgery. The first night she was in the NICU, my father remembered how important it was to do an emergency baptism if an unbaptised person was critically ill. He knocked on the entrance and asked the clerk if there was a Catholic nurse in the unit that could perform an emergency baptism. The nurse who performed the sacrament came out to tell them and exclaimed, "Monsignor Rattigan will be so proud of me!"

Father Rusty was going to perform the formal church baptism to celebrate her presence in our lives and share our happiness with all of our church family. We arranged for Father Rusty to baptize her on a Saturday afternoon, and we asked Bob and Carol to be the Godparents. They accepted the role graciously, and Carol helped Susan pick out the baptismal gown for our two—month—old little angel. The baptism was attended by over two hundred family and friends, many of whom had been praying for Christy from the day she was born. We held a potluck celebration at our new home, and the line for the buffet was out the front door and down the sidewalk. Susan and I were completely overwhelmed by the outpouring of love and care from everyone.

We were taking Christy into Kaiser monthly for check—ups with the pediatric cardiologist, who also acted as her primary pediatrician. By ten months, he was becoming concerned that she might be outgrowing her left side B—T shunt and referred her for a consult back at UCSD. We saw the pediatric cardiology fellow who had been caring for Christy during her stay after her birth. The same attending doctor also was still there, so they decided that another cardiac catheterization should be done to assess the shunt. The news wasn't good. Her shunt had narrowed to 1 mm and could close completely at any time. She needed surgery within the next couple of days to either revise it or perform another shunt on the right side.

Stunned by this assessment, we began to mentally prepare for the next chapter in the long, hard road I had been forewarned about on the night of her birth. There was a new pediatric cardiology clinical nurse specialist, or CNS, who had joined the team since our earlier stay ten months prior. Her name was Sally, and her job was to be a liaison between patients, families, and the doctors during hospitalizations and surgeries. She was a wonderful advocate for the children and a very calming influence on parents.

After we had made the plans for the surgery, Sally asked a favor of us. There was a young couple who had just delivered a baby with a severe congenital heart defect and they were having a difficult time accepting the diagnosis. Their daughter was born with transposition of the great vessels, where the left ventricle is feeding the blood to the lungs under high pressure from the left heart and the right ventricle is pumping the oxygenated blood through the aorta to the body. Their daughter, Emily Rose, also needed surgery as soon as possible, to place a temporary band around the high—pressure aorta, which was working as the main pulmonary artery. This would decrease the outflow pressure from the left ventricle and lower the high pressures being forced into the lungs. Sally arranged for us to meet the couple, Luke and Mary Ellen, in the cafeteria just to talk. They were a few years younger than us, and Emily was their first child. It was obvious from the moment we met that they were frightened, having difficulty accepting that their new baby had a major heart defect, and just needed some non—medical friends who understood what they were going through.

We talked about what we had already endured with Christy and the fact that we were looking at another surgery in the next few days. Mary Ellen wanted to know if she was a normal baby otherwise. We suggested that we take them up to see her on the pediatrics floor, and they grabbed at the chance. When we walked into the room and Christy saw Mommy and Daddy, she began jumping up and down in the crib, laughing and babbling incessantly, as she was very capable of doing. When Mary Ellen saw her, you could see all the fears melt from her body; and all she could say was, "What a beautiful little girl." We freed

Christy from the crib, and Mary Ellen wanted to hold her forever. Sally had imagined us making a huge impact on Luke and Mary Ellen, but it turned out to be Christy who made the huge impact, in reality. In no time, our daughter had shown them that a heart defect was just that, a heart defect, and from all outward appearances, she was a normal, active ten—month—old baby.

But now, it was time for us to face our worries and concerns. We brought Christy back to the medical center on a Monday to be admitted and prepared for surgery on Tuesday. With Christy older now, albeit only by ten months, it was so heart wrenching to take her into the hospital knowing the invasiveness and pain associated with what she was going to be experiencing. Susan couldn't take watching procedures being done to her baby girl without crying, so it was left to me to be the parent who stood by to calm and reassure Christy. They would take her from her hospital room into a procedure room to do such things as drawing blood and inserting IV's into her arms. It was so painful to my heart to have to hold her down with her screaming, looking into my eyes and not understanding why I would let some stranger hurt her. I kept telling myself it had to be done and to just get through it. That was the pragmatic view, but it never made it any easier to see your child in such agony and to be directly associated with making it happen.

Even worse than procedures, taking Christy to the doors of the OR and turning her over to staff for surgery provoked the greatest sense of betrayal I have ever felt. The same rationalization that it had to be done and she wouldn't be alive without her surgeries applied in a much deeper sense. However, to hug a tender toddler and say good—bye, not knowing if she would live through the surgery, was one of the worst feelings a parent could ever experience.

We took her in around 7:00 a.m. that morning and waited again in the main lobby of the hospital. This was the standard location for surgeons to find families of patients who were undergoing surgery. Both of our parents, as well as Luke and Mary Ellen and Carol and Bob, were there as moral support for us. In that situation, I could never appear upbeat or make small talk to pass the time. I wrapped myself in a shroud of worry and tried to pray my way out of it but could never reach a point of calm. Friends and family would suggest we get something to eat in the cafeteria, but I would refuse to leave the waiting area. Their solution was to bring me food, which I barely touched.

The surgery that morning was supposed to take around three hours from start to finish, so when we hadn't seen or heard from the surgeon by 10:30 a.m., my anxiety was climbing rapidly. It was around noon when Sally, the CNS, arrived. She let us know they were almost done with the operation but were leaving Christy's chest open to watch for some persistent bleeding that was going on. By mid afternoon, the cardiothoracic surgeon finally walked into the waiting room. Christy was stable and completely closed up, but they were keeping her in the recovery room for closer observation. The surgeon was unable to do a B—T shunt on the right side due to some tortuous malformations in her right subclavian artery. He had been forced to do an alternative shunt called a Waterston. This is a window that is cut between the ascending aorta and the right pulmonary artery where it runs under the aorta to the root of the right lung. This provides blood flow to both pulmonary arteries and both lungs at the tradeoff of high—pressure blood flow into the lungs. This type of shunt is not used anymore, as most recipients didn't survive it long term and most full corrections of tetralogy of fallot are now performed during infancy.

Twelve hours after we took Christy to those OR doors, the pediatric cardiologist finally came to get us at 7:00 p.m. We were told they were moving her into the pediatric intensive care unit but were still concerned over the high—pressure blood flow into her lungs and what appeared to be some developing congestive heart failure. They were leaving her intubated and on the ventilator for the time being. We were allowed to go in and see her briefly, but then we were told by the pediatric cardiologist to go home and get some rest. He would let us know if she made it through the night. I couldn't believe what he said to us. When I asked about this assessment, he replied that she was in very critical condition and just hanging on. The next twenty—four to forty—eight hours were going to be the determining factor in her outcome. I was feeling so anxious and worried after the day we had just spent, and as Susan and I sat in the waiting room, my pager went off. Without even looking at who was trying to reach me, I pulled it off my side, threw it to the floor, and tersely told Susan, "I can't do this anymore. I can't live on the edge of life and death here in the hospital and, at the same time, have to deal with stupid annoyances from running a business that doesn't matter to me."

Susan wasn't going to leave Christy alone in the hospital, so she ended up spending the night in the playroom on the pediatrics floor. This was an area that was cleared at night to provide room for parents who wanted to spend the night close to their children. We had brought a sleeping bag and pillow, anticipating that one of us would stay. She told me to go home and try to get some rest. I was so exhausted by the long day that I gladly took her up on the offer. I drove as carefully as I could from the medical center up the freeway to our house in the north city.

THE PRESENCE
OF THE SPIRIT

When I got home, I wanted to get immediately into bed. However, in our master bathroom, as I got ready for bed, I suddenly collapsed into a sobbing mess on the floor. I was completely overcome by all we had gone through and the words of the cardiologist: "I'll let you know if she makes it through the night." I was tearfully begging God to save my baby girl and let her grow up to adulthood. Suddenly, my entire body was filled with calming warmth and the sense that everything was going to be all right. Just as with Susan's conversion experience, there was no voice or visible presence but I knew without a doubt that the Holy Spirit was completely surrounding and encompassing me. The message given to me was unequivocally clear, and all my fear of her dying left me at that very moment. This experience is the most profound time in my entire life that I have known that God exists and really does answer our prayers when it follows His will, not ours. I had no doubts that His will was for Christy to grow up and live a long life.

By the next morning, Christy was doing much better and her congestive heart failure was being controlled with Lasix to remove excess fluid and Digoxin to improve her heart's contractility. They were going to extubate her, or pull the breathing tube, later that day. She also would probably be moved to a regular room from the ICU by the next day if all was going well. We were able to take her home by the end of the first week after the surgery. It felt so good to have both of our kids at home and us together again as a very blessed family.

Christy continued to do very well with the new shunt, and congestive heart failure never became a troubling issue. She steadily gained weight and, except for her blue hue to her lips and fingers, looked every bit the part of a very normal one—year—old.

HEART TO HEART

We were so happy to be able to help Luke and Mary Ellen face and conquer their fears about the future, that we came up with the idea of developing a parents' support group where all parents of children with congenital heart defects could meet other parents, their children, and get the same type of support we were able to provide Luke and Mary Ellen. We talked with Sally about the idea, and she gave us her full support to move forward. We called the group Heart to Heart and posted information for monthly meetings. Sally would also let parents know about it when they had their children in the hospital. It was an informal meeting that allowed open discussion about the same fears and worries we all had and to help each other through them. We had holiday parties and reunions of the kids who had gone through their surgeries together. At one summer picnic, we met another family who became lifelong friends. David and Denise had a daughter, Christy Lee, who had been born with tricuspid atresia, a defect where the valve between the right atrium and right ventricle didn't form.

Our friendship with Luke and Mary Ellen grew ever so strong as we supported each other through our daughters' surgeries and procedures. They moved up to the East San Francisco Bay area right after Christy's second shunt. Luke joined his mother in running a very successful party supply store, which he eventually took over and still runs to this day.

Emily had been well controlled with the banding procedure around the aorta that had been performed shortly after Christy's shunt surgery. At two years of age, it was time for Emily to go through a semi—corrective surgery called a modified Fontan procedure. The procedure was performed at UC San Francisco by one of the greatest pediatric cardiothoracic surgeons in history: Dr. Paul Ebert. Dr. Ebert had trained in cardiothoracic and general surgery at Johns Hopkins with none other than Alfred Blalock, the co—founder of the B—T shunt.

Of course, Susan and I had to be there to support Luke and Mary Ellen, so we had my parents take care of David and Christy and we flew to San Francisco.

The process of Emily's first open heart surgery took as heavy a toll on Luke and Mary Ellen as Christy's second shunt had on us. We could feel the anguish and worry they were feeling as she was admitted into the hospital and Emily went to surgery with a lot of tears being shed by all of us. After surgery, she was transferred to the ICU, and bad timing occurred as a baby boy that Mary Ellen had gotten to know before the surgery died unexpectedly while Emily was in the ICU with him. It was gut—wrenching to hold Mary Ellen as she sobbed uncontrollably in her mourning for this precious baby. She told the mother that it didn't seem fair that Emily could do so well while her baby died. I tried to reassure Mary Ellen that she had to let go and allow God to dry her tears and those of the heartbroken mother.

Emily recovered quickly, and Luke and Mary Ellen were able to take her home in about one week. She and her parents have been told over the years that no other corrective procedure is available for her heart and that she most likely will need a heart transplant at some point in time. However, she continues to go on living, able to do virtually any activity she wants, except having a baby. Without the strong bond that has built between our families over all these years, it would have been much more difficult to weather the trials of having daughters with congenital heart defects.

Prior to moving, Luke and Mary Ellen had become friends with the Asian pediatric cardiology fellow at UCSD. He had told them that Christy had coded three times in the night after her Waterston shunt. He really had not expected her to live through that night, but the Holy Spirit that surrounded me in my anguish also surrounded her in her fight to keep living. The doctor never shared this with us, and I learned this information from Luke and Mary Ellen on the night before Christy's next surgery at UCLA.

SEEDS OF CHANGE
ARE PLANTED

With everything we had been through over the prior two years, I began to feel that I was being called to do more in my life than plumbing. I really wanted to know why we had a daughter with such a defective heart and what caused it to form abnormally. I started reading as much as I could about pediatric cardiology, learned the basics of cardiac physiology, and began thinking that maybe I could make a return to school to learn medicine. I felt a burning need in my being to touch other people and make a real difference in their lives.

The seeds of change were just being planted in my life during this time. I had a really difficult time going back to running a plumbing contracting business, fighting with customers over paying their bills, and dealing with several employees who had been skimming materials and storing them in their garages to go into business for themselves. After having spent an aggregate of about three weeks dealing with life—and—death issues in the hospital during Christy's two shunt surgeries and Emily's fontan open heart procedure, I couldn't get away from that burning need I was experiencing. Most of our doctors had been very caring and thoughtful, but several had left me with the intense feeling that I could be a much better physician with more empathy and understanding than they had exhibited to us.

The turning point in my life occurred when we attended the medical school graduation of my childhood and lifetime best friend, Larry. He had finished his undergraduate studies at UCLA and began the process of applying to medical school in his final year there. It took two years of applying and interviewing, as schools were moving to expand the diversity of their students and white male applicants weren't looked at as favorably as in the past. After the second year of persistently going through the application process, he was accepted at the USC School of Medicine. I remember during his first year he invited me to go into the gross anatomy lab with him and view his cadaver dissections. I was a little apprehensive, as I had never seen a dissected body, but the intrigue and opportunity to see inside a body overwhelmed any fears I had for the visit. The experience really reinforced my feeling that I had to be doing more in my life than running a business. There were about twenty—five bodies of people who had lived lives as diverse as one could imagine, but they all felt the calling to donate their body after their death to educate physicians of the future. God only knows how many of those future physicians would treat the families and progeny of these donors without even knowing it.

At the age of twenty—seven, Larry graduated and invited the four of us to attend his graduation ceremony. I sat there as they called the roll of new graduates and awarded their medical degrees and I had the incredible realization that no matter what you are doing or where you are going, life continues on and passes far too quickly. I made the decision that day that I needed to pursue medical school. If I never tried, I would probably regret it my whole life. If I did try and failed, I could live with that much easier than not trying at all.

I talked to Susan on the drive home to San Diego about the feelings I was having and the need to pursue a drastic career change. We both knew it would be a long, difficult road that would uproot our lives and the lives of our children. How would we survive financially? Could I possibly make the transition from a tradesman with limited education to a professional with four years of graduate education and who knows how many years of residency training? And most importantly, could I even get accepted to a medical school, being six or seven years out of any post—high school education?

After a lot of prayer and reflection, together with God, we made the decision to go for it. I decided that telling others about my plans would make them reality and force me to diligently pursue them. One of the first people I told was my father. I was quite taken back by his reaction. He felt I was being foolish to give up a successful contracting business and to put my wife and children at such a risk. I told him that I had never felt more called to pursue something in my life, but it didn't change his concerns. To this day, Susan says she supported my decision to pursue medicine more because she thought I would never get into a school rather than feeling it was my calling. Nevertheless, I started looking into taking part—time classes at UCSD to meet some of the basic requirements I lacked in my undergraduate classes. I started through a program designed to provide education for returning adults. The entrance requirements were much more lenient than direct matriculation, and my lower GPA during high school wouldn't be taken as heavily into account. When I had applied for college during my senior year of high school, I was outright rejected by UCSD.

I started back slowly, taking Spanish to fulfill the one—year foreign language requirement for Muir College, the program I intended to enter at UCSD. I needed a year of physics, one year of organic chemistry, and many upper—division biology courses to complete my bachelor of sciences degree. At the rate of two classes per quarter, the maximum load I could take and still have time to run my business, it would probably take somewhere in the order of six to seven years before I could apply for medical school. This seemed like a daunting hurdle to jump, but I took it one step at a time.

THE HANDS OF A SURGEON

When Christy was four, it was time to consider doing the corrective surgery. She was still petite and barely weighed forty to fifty pounds, but her cardiologist felt it should be done before any damage was done to her lungs by the high—pressure flow of the Waterston shunt. We knew this was going to be a much more complex and lengthy surgery than her two shunts, and we asked to be able to meet with and consult several different surgeons prior to scheduling it. Dr. Ebert would not be an option, as Kaiser Permanente in Southern California did not have a contract with UCSF. Our choices were the surgeons at UCSD, San Diego Children's Hospital, and Dr. Hillel Laks at UCLA. We met with the two local surgeons in San Diego, and neither impressed us enough to feel it was a go with either one of them. One was so callous; he talked to Susan and me with Christy sitting on my lap and brought up the difficulty of the procedure, the fact she was so small, and the limited odds that she would survive. I couldn't believe he would say all of that, and never even acknowledge Christy's presence in the room.

The next week, we drove to UCLA to meet in consultation with Dr. Laks. We had an appointment to meet at 3:00 p.m. on the day of our trip to the medical center. By 4:15 p.m., his nurse came in the exam room to apologize for him being so late. We were beginning to wonder if this was the man we wanted doing our daughter's open heart surgery.

About fifteen minutes later, the door opened up and Dr. Laks entered in surgical scrubs and, ignoring Susan and I, immediately crouched down at Christy's height. She was standing in a corner of the room. He took both of her hands into his and softly spoke to her.

"Hi, Christina. I'm Dr. Laks. Do you want me to fix your heart for you?"

The decision was easily made just by that simple interaction. He apologized to us for being late, but he had been wrapping up a very complicated cardiac repair. We assured him we would have waited all night if that was what it took for him to do the right thing for his patient. The surgery was scheduled for March 21, 1985, the first day of spring that year. This also coincided with the date of my final examination in organic chemistry. I met with the professor, who agreed to let me take the exam a couple of days early, so I could leave and get to UCLA. I studied as much as I could, but my mind was on my daughter's upcoming surgery. The day I took the test, the professor had a monitor sit with me, and I just relaxed and did the best I could. I ended up acing the exam and received an A in the course. It's amazing how well you can perform when you don't really care about the outcome.

Susan and I made reservations at the university guest house, a nice hotel on campus very near to the medical center. Its primary use was for families like us with patients in the hospital. We were within walking distance to the main entrance and nearby to the arboretum, an area of lush gardens and flowers with walking trails throughout its grounds.

The surgery was to start first thing in the morning, and Christy was admitted the night before. I stayed with her that night and was allowed to sleep in a rollaway bed right next to hers. Luke and Mary Ellen showed up that night to support us, even though they hadn't indicated they were driving down from the Bay Area. I was so happy and surprised to see them. My emotions overcame me, and I began to cry. Mary Ellen took Christy out of the room to go to the playroom so she wouldn't be upset by seeing her daddy crying. I confided to Luke how hard it was this time around to send her to surgery knowing they were going to stop her heart, cool her body down, and do major surgery to build a pulmonary artery. He, of all people, understood and knew exactly what Susan and I were going through. He assured me that he and Mary Ellen would be there for us as long as we needed them. After

Christy returned with Mary Ellen, I had to give her a bath in an antibacterial disinfectant to prepare for the open heart procedure in the morning. If I slept even fifteen minutes that night, it was a miracle. I spent the whole night listening to Christy breathing and watching her chest moving up and down. I prayed through the whole night and tried to focus on that feeling of being surrounded by the Holy Spirit and the message given to me that everything would be all right on that night after her last surgery. This was only another stepping stone on the path of my beautiful daughter's lifetime.

We took her down to a similar OR door early on the morning of the twenty—first. An important addition came with us, however. Christy had a favorite pink blanket that had been with her during her last surgery. This blanket was her soothing cloth of love. She would never allow it to be washed by Susan, as there was a familiar smell to it. We asked the scrub nurse if it could go with her, and she said by all means. They would keep it on the gurney during her surgery, and it would be with her when she woke up.

This pink blanket was so important to Christy and it had almost been lost on a trip to Texas. When Kathy and Chuck's little girl, Lindsey, had been born, we decided to drive down to visit them in Corpus Christi, Texas. Chuck was stationed in Corpus during part of his six years of flight duty with the navy. He had wanted to become a commercial pilot, having already obtained his private pilot's license. At that time, the majority of pilots flying with the airlines were ex—military pilots, so Chuck thought enlisting in the US Navy would be the best way to break into the field as well as receive extensive training and flight hours toward his goal. Christy was two and a half years old at the time, and David was five and a half. We stopped in Fort Stockton, Texas, late at night, after traveling twelve hours from Tucson, Arizona. It was 9:30 p.m., and we had yet to eat any dinner, so I ran down the street to a fast food restaurant. Coming from California, I was dressed in 1980s—style men's shorts, a tank top, and flip—flops. As I walked in the entrance, all eyes in the restaurant stared me down like laser beams. The majority of the patrons inside were cowboys with jeans, boots, and cowboy hats. I've never felt so self—conscious in my life and returned to our motel room to tell Susan I was wearing my jeans the rest of the time in Texas.

The next morning, we got up at the motel, packed our bags, and started out on the highway leading to San Antonio. About three hours after we had left Fort Stockton, Christy piped up with, "Where's my pink blankie?" Pulling over to the side of the highway, we frantically searched all of the bags to no avail. We found a payphone on a side road and called the motel in Fort Stockton. I told them our daughter had left her precious pink blanket in the sheets of the bed and that we had to recover it at all costs. The clerk called the maids and they found it right where Christy had left it. I told the clerk we would be passing back in about ten days, and would pick it up if they could hold it for us.

After a great visit with Kathy and Chuck and their new daughter, Lindsey, we stopped by the motel in Fort Stockton on the way home, just as I had promised Christy. She was asleep in the backseat, taking her afternoon nap when I turned in the driveway. Suddenly, from the back, I heard her shout out, "Are we picking up my blankie, Daddy?" The maids had laundered, folded, and placed the blanket into a plastic bag for safekeeping, and the reunion with Christy was only marred by the fact that her favorite smell had been replaced by the odor of laundry detergent.

We had been told by Dr. Laks that it would be early afternoon when they would finish and he would meet us in the hospital lobby after the surgery was completed. UCLA had a similar clinical nurse specialist, and she was periodically observing from the overhead gallery and providing us with updates. As with her last surgery, Christy was having some ongoing bleeding, and it was delaying their ability to close her chest. By four in the afternoon, after nine hours of anxious waiting, we went out into a rose garden on the side of the hospital entrance and sat together on a concrete bench. We held each other and, crying together, prayed that God would let our little angel be safe and alive. Just a few minutes later, my mom, who had driven up with my dad to support us, put her head out the door and yelled to us, "Dr. Laks is here!" We rushed in to hear the news and he told us she was doing very well and was stable. He had placed a 15 mm homograft from her right ventricle and tied it into both pulmonary arteries. A homograft was an aorta taken from a cadaver, most likely another child, given the small size. It was working well and providing the flow of blood from her body and right ventricle out into the lungs. For the first time in her life, our little girl was no longer blue and had an essentially normal functioning heart. We gave Dr. Laks a tearful hug and thanked him from the bottom of our hearts for giving our daughter the chance to grow up. We both knew that God had led us to this incredible surgeon and guided his hands as he skillfully performed the complex repair of her malformed heart.

Christy was doing well post—operatively until the weekend. Her heart rate began running in the 150 range, and the covering pediatric cardiologist elected not to change anything. On Monday, when the cardiologist who had admitted her came back on duty, he asked me how long she had been running at such a fast rate. When I told him since Saturday morning, he was obviously frustrated that nothing had been done over the weekend. He informed Susan and I that Christy was in atrial flutter and would need to be cardioverted. This involved using a defibrillator synchronized to her heartbeat and shocking her back into a normal rhythm. Never having seen or experienced such a procedure, we were both very frightened. The cardiologist assured us it was low risk and was needed to slow her heart back down to a normal rate. We waited right outside the door of the ICU, and after ten minutes or so, the cardiologist called us back into the room. Christy's heart was running eighty to a hundred beats per minute and was back into a normal rhythm. She was a little groggy from the sedation they had used for the procedure but doing very well otherwise.

The day before the cardioversion, Sunday, my parents drove up to UCLA early in the morning and brought David with them. It was so good to see him, and we knew he must have felt somewhat abandoned by his mom and dad. The University's Newman Center was right across the road from the medical center. This is a Catholic center for students, and Sunday mass is held there each weekend. We all decided to go to mass together to celebrate Christy's successful surgery and pray for her recovery. During the mass, there is a prayer of the faithful where attendees of the mass could ask for prayers out loud from the congregation. My father spoke up, explaining that his granddaughter had just gone through open heart surgery and was recovering in the ICU. He asked for prayers for her, and the congregation responded with, "Lord, hear our prayer." After mass, we approached the priest who had said mass and asked if he would come over to the hospital and perform an Anointing of the Sick. Prior to the changes of Vatican II, this was Last Rites performed for those who were dying or had just died. Vatican II changed the Sacrament to the Anointing of the Sick, which could occur for any person ill and in need of God's intervention. The priest agreed to come over at 1:00 p.m. for the anointing. A young woman had been standing near us and listening to our conversation. She introduced herself as Judy and told us she was a second—year medical student. She also was a strong Catholic and asked if she could take part in the anointing that afternoon. We gratefully told her by all means, and we made plans for everyone to meet in the ICU at 1:00 p.m. When the priest arrived, we told the nurse taking care of Christy what we were planning to do and she asked if she could take part in the ceremony, too. She was a practicing Catholic and also mentioned that the pediatric intensivist working in the ICU that day was also Catholic and would probably want to take part also. There, around my sweet daughter's bed, nine of us joined hands and prayed for her healing. The priest anointed her with chrism, an oil used in the sacraments. After the anointing, Judy came with us to lunch, and we got to know her very well in a relatively short time. It turned out that she had attended a girl's Catholic school in San Diego and was a classmate of a dear friend we had at our parish in Mira Mesa. Our friend, Susie, knew Judy very well, and they still had long distance contact with each other. Susie had been one of the young adults we worked with when putting on the retreats for the youth of the church. To this day, we still exchange Christmas cards with Judy, who is a practicing internist and has four children of her own.

Christy had an extended stay at UCLA due to some concerns over possible infection and some intermittent fevers. Two days after the operation, Dr. Laks came to talk with me. It turns out that a non—sterile packing of instruments had been placed on the OR table and was used during the surgery. The instruments were clean and wrapped in a sealed package, but it just didn't say on the label that they were sterile. Because of this error, Dr. Laks wanted to keep her in the hospital post operatively for a two to three—week course of IV antibiotics and observe for any fevers. I was even more impressed with this great man. He had the courage and honesty to tell me about the error and to apologize for something that should have never happened.

We noticed that Christy seemed to be affected negatively by the long stay and closed up, not wanting to interact or talk with us. We took her for daily walks in the arboretum, and even her favorite movie, The Wizard of Oz, couldn't seem to shake her out of her funk. We finally asked Dr. Laks if she could go home over Easter weekend and be admitted down at UCSD to complete her IV antibiotics. He reluctantly agreed, and we drove home to San Diego on Holy Saturday. Easter Sunday dawned with a patented Southern California warm, sunny morning, and we decided we had to go to church. We had been told not to allow Christy to have much physical activity or be exposed to large crowds. However, we knew this was something we all had to do as a family. All of our friends and fellow parishioners were overjoyed to see Christy and enveloped her and us with gentle hugs. We even let her slowly take part in an Easter egg hunt, with lots of help from David and us. Her mood and outlook was almost back to normal, and she was actually smiling in some pictures we took in our yard. I still so treasure the photos of my pale but pink, waif—thin little angel in her pink Easter dress in our front yard.

Returning to the hospital, even though it was UCSD and close to home, was difficult for all of us, especially Christy. It seemed unfair that we had been home, enjoyed Easter, and then plunged her back into the medical environment. Fortunately, the fevers had ended, and after another twenty—four hours of IV antibiotics, we were discharged on Tuesday morning. The roughest surgery of all had been successful. Christy had survived it and now had pink lips and skin instead of blue. What a miracle God had worked through our daughter, and we were just a couple of years from seeing how that miracle was going to profoundly lead to a major change in our lives.

The week after we returned to San Diego, my business partner, Mike, informed me he wanted to go out on his own. We had diverged in the type of work we were doing. I was primarily doing new construction on custom homes and apartments while Mike had built a strong clientele of insurance companies looking for reasonable plumbing repairs when a house or building had flooding from pipe leaks. We split amicably with me operating my company, Dependable Plumbing, from home and Susan's help on the phones and accounting. Despite the sudden split, Mike and I have remained good friends over the years.

CALLED TO HEAL

In my third year back at college part—time, I did a plumbing job for a professor who was retired from the University of New Mexico School of Medicine and had moved to San Diego. When I found out his prior role, I began peppering him with loads of questions about medical school. I told him my plan to complete a BS degree in biology, and he looked at me quizzically. "Why are you finishing your undergraduate degree?" he inquired. I told him because I needed one, and he proceeded to tell me that with my life experiences of running a business, all I needed was the required courses for acceptance and I could apply without the degree. If I was a twenty—two—year—old with no life lived but school, it would be highly unlikely to be accepted to any medical school. However, for the right school, my years of working would be looked at as a positive and the admission committee would realize what a waste of time it would be for me to work to finish the undergraduate degree. This advice had just potentially saved me two to three years or more of continued part—time undergraduate courses.

The other big hurdle for me would be the Medical College Admission Test, or MCAT, that all applicants had to take and score well on to have even a chance of admission. I decided it would be worth the effort to take the preparatory course for this exam. I was scheduled to take the test before I had completed my year of physics and would be one quarter short of covering all aspects of physics. That last quarter had complex material, such as quantum mechanics, so it was up to me to learn the material in time for the test. Also, having not taken a lengthy entrance exam anytime in the past, the practice tests would be of great value. I took the real exam in the spring of 1986, and after completing it, I had no idea how I had done. It was just a relief to be finished with it, and Susan took me out to dinner to celebrate.

When the scores were mailed out, I found I had done quite well on the six subjects of basic knowledge that made up the MCAT. My pre—medical advisor at UCSD felt that, with my much—improved GPA since returning to college, I had a realistic chance of getting accepted at a school somewhere in the US.

Susan had some of her own feelings about the process, however. I could apply to any medical school in California, of which there were eight in 1986, but she didn't want to have to leave the state for me to get into medical school. I told her that approach would severely limit my chances of being accepted to a school. Her reply was that if it was God's intention for me to go to medical school, I would get accepted in California.

For the prior three to four years, while attending classes part—time, I also volunteered once a month with the pediatric cardiology group at UCSD. There was a monthly trip to Tijuana, Mexico, to Hospital Issstecali, a general hospital with a pediatrics program that was both inpatient and outpatient. I began going with Lilliam Valdez—Cruz, MD, one of the pediatric cardiologists who worked with David Sahn, MD. David is a world—renowned pediatric cardiologist who transferred to UCSD from the University of Arizona and brought many of his staff physicians, including Lilliam, with him. He is most well known for his work in ultrasound imaging of congenital heart lesions. David had become Christy's primary cardiologist at UCSD, and I had gotten to know him well. I approached him about my desire to get into medical school and my need to do some kind of volunteering to bolster my application. He suggested the Tijuana trips, and they worked perfectly to allow me to continue working, taking classes, and volunteering without taking up too much of my thin—stretched time. I learned so much about congenital heart defects, the use of ultrasound, and the need for definitive care for other children in the world. On one trip, a seriously ill infant went into cardiac arrest and I looked on as Lilliam performed CPR with no success. It was the first time I saw a patient die. In Mexico, there were children who would have been corrected at an early age if they had access to care but were living with such defects as TOF, transposition, coarctation of the aorta, and others that would progressively lead to their ultimate deaths. This experience reinforced my desire to become a doctor and try to make a difference in the lives of others. Dr. Sahn was gracious enough to also write a letter of recommendation for my application process. Applicants were not allowed to read their recommendation letters, but one of my interviewers commented that it was the strongest letter of advocacy he had ever read.

My rounds of interviews began in fall of 1986, and the first was at USC. It probably didn't hurt that Larry had written a letter of recommendation on my behalf. I received outright rejection letters from UCLA, UCSF, and Stanford as well as Loma Linda University. My chances of getting into medical school were now down to half of the California schools, with USC, UC Irvine, UCSD, and UC Davis still possibilities. The next two interviews were at UC Irvine and at UCSD. San Diego was my wishful top choice, as our home, family, and my daughter's medical care were all there locally. UCSD had a process of initially interviewing their applicants through the pre—medical advising office to assess the likelihood they would be offered direct interviews with the admission committee. I met with the advisor completing the interview and told her about my daughter's health issues and how important it was that we remain in San Diego for her future care. The advisor's response was, "I wouldn't advise that you tell a faculty interviewer any of that information. UCSD only wants 100—percent—committed applicants who are willing to sacrifice everything for admission to the school." I was completely abhorred that another person would say something like that to me. My daughter and her health were a very high priority in my life, and if that was the prevailing attitude at UCSD, I wouldn't want to be a student at the medical school.

In the early part of October, I received notice that I had been selected for an interview at UC Davis. I had never been to Davis but had spent lots of time in Sacramento with an uncle, aunt, and cousins who had lived there for many years. We drove through Davis on the way to visit other relatives in the Bay area, but the only thing I knew about it was that the campus was world renowned for its veterinary medicine school. I also knew an older brother of Susan's friend and former roommate, Diana, who had attended law school at Davis. I arranged for a flight from San Diego to Sacramento early in the morning the day of the interview. I was scheduled to meet in the late morning with two interviewers, one a medical school professor and the other a third—year student on the admissions committee. Both interviews were on the campus of the UC Davis Medical Center near downtown Sacramento. I arrived at the hospital and checked in with the student affairs office. The student I was scheduled to meet with had cancelled, and a second—year student had been assigned in her place. I felt a little awkward selling myself to a person no older than maybe twenty—three when I was nine years older and much more experienced in life. The student was very pleasant and highly interested in hearing about my experience running my own business for twelve years. I also was able to captivate her with stories of monthly trips to the Children's hospital in Tijuana, Mexico, as a volunteer with the pediatric cardiology group at UCSD Medical Center. I was able to assist with cardiac echoes on the hearts of children who had never had the opportunity for medical care or corrective surgeries. I also related the story to her of a three—year—old child who desperately needed access to a major heart center, such as UCLA. Lilliam had talked with the mother, who had relatives in Los Angeles and could stay with them during the surgery. The only problem was the child had to appear in person via the ER to get coverage via Medi—Cal or CCS funding. Lilliam had asked me if I knew how she could get the child to LA without being turned back by the border patrol. I drew her a detailed map of some roads winding through the area of north San Diego County that would bypass the two major immigration checkpoints on I—5 and I—15. Once in LA, Lilliam could get the child admitted to the ER and arrange for her to have life—saving emergency surgery. The student interviewer was astounded that I had done this to save a child. When the interview was finished, I felt it had gone extremely well and told the student I appreciated her taking her time out of a rigorous schedule to fill in for my interview.

The next interview was with a professor in the Department of Family Practice, Walter Morgan, MD. Dr. Morgan and I hit it off right away, partly because there was remodeling and expansion going on in the outpatient family medicine clinic and he was amazed at how familiar I was with the building process. He also seemed to be genuinely interested in my reasons for being willing to give up a lucrative business for the long process of medical school and residency. Not knowing his position on religion or faith, I took a chance and told him that I felt I had been called by God to do more with my life and I did not want to look back at the end of it all and say I ran a business, made lots of money, and lived comfortably without striving to reach for a higher goal. I shared with him all the hospital experiences with my daughter and the life—and—death moments I saw around us when in the grip of her medical problems. He seemed impressed and told me he was very grateful I had applied to and considered Davis for medical school. This was so counterintuitive to what I had heard from the advisor at UCSD.

Dr. Morgan explained to me that the first two years of medical school at Davis were spent at the Medical Sciences building in Davis and the last two here at the hospital campus. He suggested that I drive my rental car back through Davis, which was only fifteen miles west of Sacramento. I could then take a road out of the college town north to the airport for my flight home to San Diego. He drew me a detailed map and even suggested some areas in Davis to look around to get the flavor of the campus and downtown area. He then took me to an office where a staff member of his department sat at a desk. She and her husband had come to Davis with a family, as we would if I was accepted there. The woman was very kind, told me about her husband, who was now an intern in OB—GYN at the medical center, and provided their phone number so we could contact them for a visit if I was accepted. I thanked both her and Dr. Morgan for their genuine interest and hospitality during my visit. I found my rental car in the parking structure and began the drive west to Davis.

When I left the I—80 freeway at the Davis off ramp, I drove under a railroad bridge and into a cute downtown with lots of shops. I followed the campus loop road that rounded its way past the famous Davis water tower, past cows, horses, and sheep being studied by agriculture students and veterinary students, and to the Medical Sciences building at the west end of campus.

I still had several hours until my flight to San Diego, so I drove through some of the older neighborhoods north of campus. I was struck by how familiar the town felt even though I had never been in Davis in the past. I didn't know if it was because it reminded me of Brawley and Calipat from my childhood or why it seemed so familiar. I also had an overwhelmingly distinct feeling that I was going to be accepted to medical school at Davis and that this small campus town was going to be my new home in the near future.

When I arrived home at our house in San Diego, I couldn't shake this continued feeling of familiarity and future life in Davis. It was so strong that the first words I uttered to Susan after kissing her hello were, "Well, are you ready to move to Davis?"

This took her by surprise, and I shared with her my experiences during the day and the intense feelings I was having about it. She still wanted me to pursue getting admitted to UC San Diego, which I promised her I would do. It certainly would be much easier on us as a family not to pull up our roots; leave our church where we were so involved and known; and make our children attend new schools in a strange, new town. I even had thoughts, however unrealistic, that I could continue to supervise employees of our plumbing company during medical school and have some continued income to support the family and pay the school fees.

Over the next week, I heard back from USC and was informed that I was on the waiting list to fill a spot if enough students accepted admission at other schools. I continued working, just waiting to hear back from UCSD.

On Halloween evening, October 31, 1986, I got home late after a very dirty job laying new piping in trenches. I was muddy, wet, and on the side of the garage trying to get the mud off my pants and boots the best I could. Susan suddenly opened the door to the house from the garage and yelled, "Mike, come quick. It's Dr. Morgan from UC Davis." I threw off my shoes, ran into the house, and grabbed the phone. Breathlessly, I said, "Hi, Dr. Morgan. I was just cleaning up after a messy day at work." He made some small talk, asking about how my business was going and where things were in my interviewing process. He then astounded me when he broke the news that I had been accepted to medical school at UC Davis to enter the class that would start in fall 1987 and graduate in June 1991. Stunned, I thanked him through tearful eyes and listened to him tell me how impressed the admissions committee had been by my story and the reasons for wanting to be a doctor. After finishing the call, I screamed to Susan, "I'm going to be a doctor!" I immediately set about calling my parents, who were very happy for me, and also called other family members as well as Larry and Gail. I told Larry my fears, that as this elusive butterfly was now netted, I would be much less educated than my classmates, many of whom might have PhD's, research backgrounds, or nursing education as their backgrounds before medical school. Here I was, a lowly plumber and businessman. He reassured me that the first two years were going to be a lot of review of sciences I already had taken and that medical schools did everything they could to help make sure all students passed the courses and eventually graduated. He then asked me, "Know what they call the medical student who graduates last in his or her class?" I had no idea, and replied so. "Doctor," was his response.

That night, we took the kids out trick—or—treating after dinner. Every neighbor who asked how we were, I told them of my great news. It was hard to believe that in just under a year, I would be a student in medical school.

We lay in bed that night and talked about all of the excitement and implications of such a major life change. I felt a bond with UC Davis, especially with all the nice comments made by Dr. Morgan. San Diego, however, was still our top choice. I had interviewed at UCSD the week before the Davis trip but had not heard anything yet. This was not the least unusual, as some students receive their acceptance as late as the beginning of September, a few weeks before the start of school.

It was going to be a dilemma for us, however, as a family. If we had to move to Davis, many plans had to be made in a relatively short period of time. The plumbing business would have to be dealt with and either sold or a strong manager put in place to run it in my absence. My cousin, Craig, had gone to work with me about three to four years earlier. He had grown tired of working as a tuna fisherman and taking long trips down the coast of Central and South America as the captain and crew chased schools of tuna in the blue Pacific Ocean. Craig was one of the hardest—working men I had ever met and had been promoted to lead skiff boat runner. These were the small boats complimenting the massive purse seiner tuna boat. The skiffs would hook onto the immense purse nets and drag them out and around a school of fish. As the nets were dragged in and slowly lifted as well as tightened around the large schools, the skiff boat drivers often had to jump into the writhing mass of tuna to remove dolphins in an attempt to save them from a crushing death. This was dangerous work, as sharks, some as big as 12 to 15 feet were also inadvertently hauled in with the tuna. It required a keen eye to make sure your leg or body was not within striking distance of a very angry trapped shark. When Craig approached me about learning plumbing and giving up the months long trips at sea, I happily took him on as a protégé. He was a quick study and willing to do any work necessary to complete a job.

Over the next few weeks after receiving my news of acceptance at UC Davis, I talked with Craig about the possibility of buying the business and continuing to run it after I left. He was eager for the opportunity but thought it might work better with a partner. Another employee, Tony, had come to work with us to also learn plumbing a couple of years prior to this time. Tony had worked with his brothers building houses and apartment buildings, and their company had provided a lot of business for me. Tony was tired of working high up on framed units, lifting rafters, beams, and other heavy construction materials onto second or third stories and roofs. He was having chronic back pain and hoped a change of trade would give him greater longevity in the construction business.

Craig and Tony worked well together, and Craig felt he was a natural to take on as a partner. I agreed, and we began negotiating the sale. I wanted a steady flow of cash during my four years of school but wanted it to be reasonable payments so as not to break the success of the business. They each paid $5,000 down, and the business would make monthly payments of $500 per month for the next four years. I also was keeping my accounts receivable up to the date of transfer, which amounted to close to $100,000 dollars. The plan was for me to transfer the business to Craig and Tony effective July 1, 1987. Between October 1986 and the planned transfer, I worked almost sixty hours per week and was able to net almost $300,000 in an eight—month period. This was the security I needed to feel I could take care of my family. I could also spend four years in medical school without a job while at the same time paying the fees each quarter and paying for numerous textbooks and equipment. My goal was to complete the four years of school without taking any student loans.

We made plans to visit Davis as a family over the Thanksgiving weekend a few weeks later. We had an afternoon dinner with our families and then left San Diego in the late afternoon. We drove until Buttonwillow, a small town along I—5 in the central valley and roughly the halfway point between San Diego and Davis. The night was spent at a motel there, and then we got up early Friday morning to finish the drive north to Davis. Arriving around 10:00 a.m., we drove through the town and around the campus loop to allow Susan and the kids to see what I had seen when I made my interview trip. The weather was miserable this day, however, as the central valley's famous tule fog had settled in from Fresno to above Sacramento.

Prior to the trip, I had contacted the staff member, Karen, that Dr. Morgan had introduced me to during my interview. She had suggested at that time that if we wanted to come up, we could hook up and even spend the night at their house. Our plan was to visit with them for a couple of hours and then proceed on to the east Bay community of Alamo, where Luke and Mary Ellen live. We had really wanted to see them and would spend Friday and Saturday night with them and then drive the entire distance back to San Diego on Sunday.

Karen's husband, Jerry, was coming off of night call and looked dead tired, lying on their couch in his scrubs and socks. The two of them had a lot of good suggestions regarding neighborhoods to look at, the excellent Davis school system for the kids, and survival tips for medical school. Jerry also allayed my fears of being the lowest in the class, given my plumber's background. He said that UC Davis in particular worked very hard on accepting students with diverse backgrounds and did everything they could to make sure each student graduated.

Jerry had been diagnosed in his first year of medical school with Hodgkin's lymphoma, and took a year off for treatment and recovery. He had been in remission for almost four years and was tired but very happy to be starting his residency training. After a couple of hours of hearing about how good life was in Davis for their family, we thanked them for the hospitality and jumped back in the car for the short trip to Alamo.

As it always is, it was so good to see Luke and Mary Ellen. We caught up with our lives and talked about where our daughters' health was at currently. Both girls, Christy and Emily, were at stable points in their health lives, neither taking any medications and no procedures or surgeries planned for the foreseeable future. Emily was still most likely going to need a heart transplant eventually but, for the time being, was playing soccer and keeping up with her numerous friends. Christy had wanted to join soccer, but we were worried, probably overly so, that she might be at risk for getting hit in the chest. Her aortic homograft put in at UCLA bulged at the front of her sternum. It most likely would have been safe, but we preferred that instead of sports she pursue a safer activity, such as playing the piano. We had started her with lessons about a year previously, and she really took to playing it. Catching up was easy after not seeing Luke and Mary Ellen for a few years, and it was like we hadn't been living at opposite ends of California. On Saturday morning, we decided we wanted to begin the trip home to avoid the horrible I—5 traffic going back to LA on the Sunday of Thanksgiving weekend. As we drove south, we talked about Davis and how, as a small college town, we could be very comfortable there. Given all that, it still would be easier, we thought, to get accepted at UCSD and not have to uproot our family. The wait was on to hear back from UCSD.

A MOTHER'S SECRET

During my last year of part—time classes at UCSD, family issues developed with my Grandma. She had slowly been showing signs of probable Alzheimer's dementia, forgetting names and dates and becoming generally confused. She lived by herself in an old house that had been owned by her second husband. When my grandfather had died in 1969, she had taken caregiver jobs cooking, cleaning, and watching over elderly adults much older than her. Her last position was with a widower, Bert, who was fifteen years her senior. At eighty—five, he was still very spry and doing jobs around the house, such as climbing up on the roof of the house to move or adjust the TV antenna. He also had a duplex where the front unit was leased for rental income. He grew to depend on my grandmother and asked her to marry him. She had been lonely since the loss of my grandpa, so she accepted the proposal. They had several years together that were happy for Grandma, but Bert passed away and left her alone again.

I tried to visit her as often as I could, but with the business, and two children, it wasn't as often as it should have been. My mother and Aunt Greta had been concerned about a couple of guys who lived two doors up the street from her. They were a gay couple who seemed to be very talented at taking advantage of lonely, elderly people. In fact, when I heard they had talked Grandma out of $2,000 to pay for some expenses, I started dropping by frequently in between jobs to check on her. One morning, I knocked at the door and it was answered by one of the men. Telling him I was there to visit with my grandma, I asked him to step out of the house and leave. He complied with my request and left only after saying, "I'll see you later, Grandma." This irritated me to no end since they were not family and obviously were taking advantage of her loneliness. I began talking with Grandma, explaining that these two guys were taking advantage of her and she needed to make sure she didn't give them any more money. Suddenly, the other guy walked out of the hallway. He had been using her shower when I arrived and had been listening to my conversation with Grandma. I got so angry at him I didn't know what to say. I told him to get out of the house and for him and his partner to never contact my grandmother again. If I ever found them in her house again, I would drag them out using a pipe wrench to motivate them. My mother and aunt went to court to obtain a restraining order and also took them to small claims court to recoup the $2,000. They had no money or jobs, so collecting it was not going to happen.

I really became concerned about Grandma when, one day, I stopped by to visit and she didn't answer the knock on the door. I looked around for an open door or window, and the only access I could find was a second—story window in the back of the house above her desk. I was in my small pickup truck and didn't have a ladder with me. I looked around the yard and found an old, long, wooden ladder lying along the side of the two houses. I propped it up against the backside of the house just under the open window. Nervously, I began to climb up the ladder toward the window. I was mostly worried about the integrity of the ladder and didn't want to fall off of it two stories up. I also, however, was worried about what I might find when I got into the house. Grandma was always very good about answering the door, so part of me worried she might be dead inside the house. I got to the window and was able to remove the screen. I looked in and yelled out to her but didn't get a reply. There was a faint sound like someone talking, but I couldn't tell where it was coming from in the house. I cautiously pulled myself into the window and stepped onto an open area on the top of her desk. Jumping down onto the rug on the floor, I began to search the house. Looking into the kitchen, I didn't see her, even though this was the place she was most likely to be. I could now hear her voice, talking to someone in one of the back bedrooms. Maybe she was on a phone call with a friend or family member and hadn't heard my knocking and yelling. I walked back into the bedroom where I could hear the voice, and there was my grandma, talking into the mirror over the dresser.

I was frightened by what I was witnessing but asked her, "Grandma, who are you talking with?"

My voice startled her, but she sheepishly told me, "I'm talking with my friend."

"Who's your friend?" I asked.

Pointing to her image in the mirror, she said in a matter—of—fact manner, "She is."

That was the final straw for me. We had been talking as a family about getting her into a care facility, but it had not happened as of yet. I told Grandma I was going to pack some of her clothes and personal items and take her to my house. She jumped at the chance to go somewhere and be around family. I loaded everything and her into my plumbing truck, and we drove to my house in Rancho Penasquitos. When we got to the house, I began making calls to several assisted living facilities and found one with an opening. It was located in the Clairemont area close to both my mother and Greta. We took it sight unseen and moved Grandma in the next day. She seemed to do better in the social environment of the facility and enjoyed talking to others of her generation.

It was clear that there was no way she could ever return to living in her home, so all of the immediate family gathered one weekend to remove all of her belongings and furniture from the house. Bert had written into his will that Grandma could live in the house for the rest of her life but that ownership of the property would go to his daughters from his first marriage when Grandma left or died. It took us well over three days to clear everything out. Most of her old furniture we either divided among the family or donated. My mother had the task of going through her papers and photographs. Late on the last day of clearing the house, my mom handed me a plastic bag with twenty to thirty old family photos. I took the bag and dropped it into the glove compartment of my truck. I took some of the small items to Grandma's new room at the care facility and then trudged home to a hot shower and bed.

Those old photos sat in my glove box for several weeks until I ran into them while cleaning up the vehicle. I pulled them out and began to casually leaf through them. Most were taken at the old company house on the canal down in Calipat. They were shots of my mom as a twenty—something young woman with me, my uncle Bob, or my grandfather. One in particular caught my eye. It was my great—grandmother standing with Grandma, Mom, and me at about two years old. For no obvious reason, I turned the photo over, and there on the back were the names of everyone in the photo. It appeared to be my grandma's handwriting and read "Jesse Howland (my great—grandmother), Alene Baird (Grandma), Shirley Baird, and Michael Gibson." Gibson? But my name was Michael Carl. Then it dawned on me and I ran into the house to show it to Susan. As I handed it to her, I stated that my father whom I had known since the age of four was not my biological father. I had always sensed that this might be the case but never had any confirmation of this sense until then. My father was absent the first years of my life, and I had known my grandfather as DaDa. My father always seemed to have more love and affection for my little sister, Lisa; but as I grew up, I noticed this seemed to be true of all father—daughter relationships, so didn't make much of it.

Susan, as baffled as I was why we had never known this, drove right away to the escrow office my aunt Greta owned and where Susan worked part—time. She walked into Greta's office and, handing her the photo, asked her what this meant. Greta looked at the photo and said it was a photo of Grandma Howland, Grandma Alene, Shirley, and Mike.

"No. Turn it over and read it," Susan replied.

When Greta read my name, she put her head into her hands and could only mutter, "Oh Lord!"

When she had gotten over the shock of reading the back of the photo, she told Susan, "I can't explain everything. Mike is going to need to talk to his mom."

Susan returned home and related her conversation with Greta to me. By then, I was confused and angry and didn't understand why I was finding this out at the age of thirty years old. I called Greta at the office and explained that I would talk with my mom when the time was right but I needed to know one thing from her. I told her I could accept that my father was not my real father, but I would be devastated if my mother wasn't my real mother. She confirmed that she was my one and only mother but said that the rest of the story had to come from my mom.

I spent a couple of days in confusion and wondering how this changed who I was and who my family was that I had known my entire life. It was so incredible that all I could do was look to God to help me through it. How was I going to talk with my mom about something so deep and secret for so many years? Why didn't they tell me when I was old enough to understand it? This was something that affected primarily me, yet all the rest of my family knew about it and had kept it from me my entire life.

I called my mother on a Thursday, two days after I had found the photo. I didn't know if Greta had forewarned her that I knew, but if she did, my mom did a very good job of hiding it. I talked casually and told her I was going to be at the library late on Friday evening and if I could I'd like to join her and my dad for dinner that night. She said sure and asked me if I wanted anything in particular.

"No," I replied. "Just surprise me."

I prayed that whole day that God would show me how to have this talk with my parents because I couldn't do it alone. I drove up to their house around 6:30 p.m., never having really been at the library, and we sat down at the table since dinner was all ready. We ate and made small talk. They asked me about my classes and how the business was doing. It was tense for me, but they didn't seem nervous or anxious. It was as though they didn't know where the conversation was going to lead.

I had the photo in my jacket pocket and would pull it out at the right time. I started slowly, telling them that I didn't just come over to have dinner. Taking a breath, I looked at my mom, and said, "God has really been working in my life the past few years. With Susan's near—death, Christy's heart defect and surviving three surgeries, and with my calling to work toward medicine, He has guided all of us through tough times and great times. Mom, he was also working through you when you handed me the plastic bag that contained this photograph."

I pulled the photo from my pocket and handed it to her. She turned it over, saw the writing on the back, and burst into tears. "I've wanted to tell you for so long but just didn't know how to do it," She cried. "I even prayed in the Basilica of our Lady of Guadalupe during our vacation to

Mexico City. I asked the Virgin Mary to guide me and help me reveal this secret to you," she tearfully told me.

"Well, she answered your prayers with this photograph," I told her.

I hugged her tightly and told her it was all okay. I looked over at my father, who hadn't said anything through all of this difficult conversation. He had a look of sorrow on his face. I walked around to him and hugged him as well.

"Dad, being a father isn't about making a woman pregnant. It's about loving a child, watching them grow up, sitting by their side when they're running a fever and sick, and teaching them how to be a good person. It's about teaching them your faith in God and seeing their first communion in the church. You've done all that for me, Dad, and you will always be my father, no matter what the DNA shows."

We talked for a couple of hours, and the whole story came pouring out.

My mother had been engaged to a young man, Neil, who had joined the US Navy and been deployed overseas. She broke off her engagement with Neil when he left, not wanting to be alone and waiting several years for his return. She knew my biological father and, with the encouragement of his mother, began a dating relationship. As fate would have it, she became pregnant with me during a weekend trip to San Diego with him. She had been encouraged by our family to give me up for adoption, but she refused, wanting to keep her baby. My biological father denied that he was the one who had impregnated my mom and cut off all contact with her. That night, during the telling of the story, my mom offered me the information to be able to contact him, but I told her no, that he made his position known from the moment I was born. No good could come from me contacting him all those years later. Besides, my father was right here with us. My father had been the impetus to keep it secret all these years. He wanted me to grow up believing fully that he was my father and felt that if I knew the truth I wouldn't love him. Both of them had worried through the years that my grandma would reveal the secret to me.

"Well, she did," I told them, "in the way God intended for it to happen."

My mother had scoured all her photos before that day we cleaned out the house, removing any that referred to me as Michael Gibson, but she missed that one critical picture with the writing on the back. I told them that in some ways, I was better off finding out at thirty rather than as a child or teenager. Having two children of my own and going through Christy's medical issue had taught me the true meaning of being a father.

Nothing was kept secret in the Imperial Valley, and Neil found out that my mother was pregnant. He sent word through a friend that he still wanted her and would marry her if she would put his name on my birth certificate. Additionally, he wrote her a letter saying that he was still willing to marry her and take me as his own son. She never received the letter, never heard any more from Neil, and carried on with her life. When my mother met Paul Lavon Carl, my stepfather, at the Catholic Church in Calipat, she found that he was willing to love her and her young son just the same. They were married when I was almost four years old, and I have distant recollections of being at the wedding. I could never understand that until finding out the story of the secret. Then everything began to make sense. A distant memory of sitting in my mother's lap in a court of law was the adoption hearing in Imperial County Court. The first four years of my life without a father were now very clear.

That day of cleaning out my grandma's belongings also revealed more than my fatherhood. My mother found the letter from Neil. It had been intercepted by Grandma and hidden for decades. For whatever reason, she didn't want my mother to see it and hid it until that fateful day it was found. He wrote that he loved her no matter what happened and would still marry her if she would have him. I can only attribute it to God's will of how, where, and with whom I would grow up.

In the early 1950s, Mexico was a place pregnant teenage girls could look to obtain an abortion to save the shame of an illicit pregnancy for their family and themselves. I have thanked my mother many times since learning the story for not looking to that as an option. It took tremendous courage for her to have a baby at nineteen and work as a single mother to raise me. This is a debt of gratitude I can never fully repay.

I still wonder about the other family to which I am related. I apparently have three other half sisters I have never met and who knows how many aunts, uncles, and cousins. I still feel, however, that it would serve no good purpose to contact any of them at this point in my life. My biological father's sister, my paternal aunt, has kept in touch with my mom and is aware of the major milestones in my life. She readily accepted that her brother was my biological father even if he never could.

FROM PARENTHOOD TO PHYSICIANHOOD

This chapter name is actually the title of a journal article I wrote and got published in my first year of medical school. It appeared as the human interest section in the Western Journal of Medicine and described the medical procedures my daughter had endured and how the experiences led me to the calling of becoming a physician.

By spring of 1986, I still had not heard news from UCSD, so I contacted the school of medicine's admission office. The admission clerk looked over my file and provided her assessment of my status. She told me that I was on the wait list and most likely would be accepted there but it could be as late as a week before the start of classes. I explained that I had already been accepted at UC Davis back in October and that, if I couldn't have a more concrete answer, I would have to withdraw my application at UCSD. There was nothing she could do to expedite my status, so I asked her to remove my name from the waiting list. This actually was a relief to me in that I knew where I would be attending medical school. Susan supported this action, and we made plans to complete the four years and hopefully move back to San Diego for residency training. I also was now able to set up the sale of the plumbing company as planned and could focus my energies on getting ready to move, getting our house in San Diego leased, and finding a house in

Davis. Not knowing the real estate market there, we decided we would rent a house for the four years of school and then move back into our San Diego home for residency if all went as planned.

Over the Fourth of July weekend, we took a trip to Davis to locate housing. We had a travel trailer we had bought a few years prior that we used for camping trips. I located a KOA Campground in West Sacramento, about 10 miles east of Davis. We towed it up with us on the Thursday night before the Saturday holiday. We spent the first night in a campground along I—5 and arrived at the KOA in the early afternoon on Friday. The best part was that they had an RV storage area and we would leave our trailer there to save having to tow it to Northern California again when we moved.

We got up early on Saturday morning, July 4, to begin our search for a nice rental house to lease. Not being very familiar with Davis, other than the information we had gotten over Thanksgiving from Jerry and Karen, we ran into numerous obstacles. The first was that there is an annual bicycle race through downtown Davis every year, so the streets are closed off and most of the realty offices are shut down at least during the morning race. We were able to find several that were open, and part of their business was leasing houses to the transient student population. Armed with some addresses and a map of the city, we set out to look for a potential home for the next four years. This was the first experience with rental property since our late teens when we both moved out of our parents' houses. We saw everything from overpriced large houses that were out of our league, to forty—year—old places that had been rentals for decades and looked like it. The other problem we were facing was that we had our first baby, Kimba, the shaggy—haired mutt we had rescued as a puppy from the San Diego Humane Society. She was twelve years old and we had to be able to keep her with us, lest the kids and us be devastated.

By Saturday night, we were tired of walking through dirty houses, and the kids wanted to see the fireworks that Davis hosts at the community park every Fourth of July. We found a Mexican food restaurant, La Esperanza, which was located in an old renovated hotel at the corner of Second and G streets downtown. We walked in to a dimly lit eatery with wooden floors that reminded me of Hussong's Cantina in Ensenada, Mexico. Thankfully, it was missing the beer on the floor and drunken touristas dancing on the tables. The food turned out to be pretty good, although nothing to compare with some of the restaurants in Old Town San Diego. The margaritas worked just fine, however, and we finally could catch our breaths.

We talked about how disappointed we were in what we had seen that day for housing options, and we even considered selling our house in San Diego and buying a house in Davis. The resale housing market wasn't much better than the lease offerings, as there were no new developments in Davis. We decided to quit worrying about it and that we would enjoy the fireworks after dinner. We would begin our search anew on Sunday morning after getting some rest.

The annual fireworks display is a heritage of the city of Davis and has been for decades. The festivities start in the mid morning at Community Park with baseball and soccer games, booths for food and drink, and swimming competitions in the public pool. The park is located a mile or so north of downtown and is a massive area of grass, sports complexes, and the pool. It is just adjacent to Davis Senior High School, so the extent of the area appears much larger than it actually covers. There are numerous tennis courts open free to the public year round and a beautiful performing arts venue, the Veteran's Center. We arrived before sunset, and David and I found an open area to kick his soccer ball around. Little did we know that soccer is a big sport for Davis kids, and we soon had several young boys wanting to join us. Susan and Christy had staked out an area to see the fireworks. The rockets were set up in a vacant field between the park and the high school. When they went off a little after 9:00 p.m., we were treated to best display we had ever seen in our lives. It was a nice way to end an otherwise disappointing day.

We got up Sunday morning and left the trailer after eating some breakfast. We found more realty companies open after the holiday and started out to look around. An agent from one company went with us and took us into some unusual houses. The construction design in Davis was not something that mirrored San Diego. One house had an overgrown atrium as you entered the front door. Many had only carports and no garages. When the agent showed us one with no air conditioning, he tried to make us believe you didn't need air conditioning in Davis. You just opened all the windows and the breezes from the Sacramento—San Joaquin Delta were natural air conditioning. Most of the rentals were listed for $900—$1200, much more than we were planning on spending. By the afternoon, after stopping for lunch, we decided to check out one more realty office and then seriously consider buying a house to own for the four years. On a bulletin board just outside the front door was a list of rentals. One, a three—bedroom, two—bath older house, had just been added on Saturday evening. We jotted down the address and drove to the house in the mid afternoon. When we pulled up, we were stunned by the size of the yard. It was located on a rounded corner of the street and had numerous mature trees in both the front and backyards. We walked up and knocked on the door, but there was nobody at the house. From a large front porch, we looked into the living room and saw a fairly large room with one wall covered by a large brick fireplace. The interior looked like it had been freshly painted, and there was new carpeting and linoleum in the parts of the house we could see through windows. We thought we must have made an error and this house was for sale, not rent. There was a phone number on a flyer taped to one of the windows, so I left Susan at the house and drove to a gas station to call the owner. It turns out she was upgrading everything after some longtime renters had recently vacated the house. I told her about my acceptance to medical school and our plan to rent for four years. When I asked the monthly rent, I almost fainted when she told me it was $850 per month. This place was perfect. It was in an older but well—established area of Davis and was one of the neighborhoods Karen had put at the top of her list for us to search. I told the owner we would take it and asked if she could meet us at the house that evening. She came over and opened it up for us to see the inside, and we wrote her a check for the first month's rent and the deposit. She also was willing to allow us to bring Kimba as long as we didn't bring her into the house. We signed a "Davis model lease" which is used in the town for students looking to live during the school year and move home during the summer. I told her we would be there at least four years for medical school. Leaving that evening to go back to the KOA, we couldn't believe how fortunate we were to find such a beautiful place completely refurbished and in move—in condition. God had taken care of us, and we had a new home to call our own for four years.

MOVING NORTH
TO A NEW LIFE

We spent the rest of July getting our house leased and packing up all of our furniture and belongings. We had a moving company transport all of the large furniture and boxes, and we towed a U—Haul trailer filled with our houseplants, cleaning equipment, and sleeping bags. We were arriving a few days before the movers, so we were going to have to camp out in our bedrooms until the furniture arrived.

Saying good—bye to the business, our family, and our friends was a very bittersweet experience. We were excited and looking forward to our new life, but the uncertainty of the new college town, new neighbors, and new friends made all of us a little anxious. San Diego was where we both had grown up from the age of five, and we had lived our entire lives there. Both of our children were born there and had never lived anywhere else.

When we left the house, we drove by Gail and Larry's home to say good—bye to them. They had bought a new house just a few blocks from ours several months before. Tears were shed, hugs were given all the way around, and promises were made to see each other regularly.

The drive up north was uneventful, and we stopped halfway at a motel in Buttonwillow, our favorite halfway stop. We took our old dog, Kimba, in the back of my Toyota 4—Runner and let her out every couple of hours at the motel to do her business and stretch her legs. We arrived late morning on August 1, 1987 and found out how different the summer was compared to the Thanksgiving trip and even the recent July 4 trip. August 1st was a hot, dry day with still air and no wind. We set about cleaning the house, as cobwebs had developed since we saw it one month prior. The first thing I noticed was how prevalent spiders, especially daddy long legs, were in Davis compared with San Diego. My first purchase at the local Ace Hardware Store was a Webster, a round—headed broom for brushing away spiders and cobwebs. After sunset, we opened the windows and realized the agent who told us you didn't need air conditioning in Davis was partially right. The delta breezes blew in, coming up the Sacramento River and the Yolo Bypass, a large overflow area reinforced with levees to store excess water from the river during winter months. It really was like natural air conditioning, as the agent had said. The only problem was that during the day, temperatures up to 105–110 F required continuous use of the air conditioner until sunset arrived. The next few days were spent waiting on the moving van and then arranging our furniture and beds when it arrived. We had left our refrigerator and washer/dryer for the new tenants in San Diego, as our new Davis rental house was equipped with all appliances. I didn't start school until the end of September, so we had a lot of nice time to get to know the community and our new home. There was a big, old oak tree in the backyard, and I spent a good part of the time off building the kids their first real treehouse. There was a ladder up the trunk to a trap door that opened onto the platform of the house. I added a large wooden railing all the way around, as it ended up about twelve feet off the ground and didn't want any broken arms or worse from my handiwork. Friends of ours from San Diego, Bob and Sue, came up toward the end of August, and we all took a trip to Lake Shasta to camp and fish. Both families had travel trailers that we had used on trips together around Southern California. I had bought an inflatable boat with an outboard motor down in San Diego, so we spent a week heading out onto the lake each day, swimming, fishing, and water skiing behind the inflatable.

Susan had started immediately applying for jobs at the university right after we had moved into the house and got several interviews before the Shasta trip. While on Lake Shasta, one department manager called her to offer her a position. It was working in the accounts payable department for the whole university, processing thousands of bills and accounts payables generated every month. We talked about it while at Lake Shasta and together decided she should accept the position since she hadn't heard back from any of the other departments.

Susan started the job on August 31 and quickly grew to dislike the manager and the environment. The department used antiquated pen tabs to enter all of the accounts payable into the system by hand. You had to have specific ways of entering characters or the pad would read the entry incorrectly. Any error was considered egregious by the manager, yet she demanded speed and productivity on the part of all employees.

Susan came home in tears on numerous occasions; and worse, she had received interview call backs from a number of the other departments she had applied to for a job. The university required a six—month probation period before you could apply for or change jobs. Her first priority when the six months was up was to change jobs to a better department.

I started classes at the end of September after attending a really nice welcome breakfast. A majority of the medical school faculty was in attendance, and the welcome ceremony was held outside on the lawn between the Med Sciences Lab building and our lecture hall. The first quarter schedule was a few smaller classes such as embryology, introduction to radiology, and immunology. The major course for the first quarter was human anatomy. This was an entire quarter of learning every bit of the anatomy of the human body through didactic lectures and hands—on dissection of a donated cadaver. There were four students per cadaver, and we took turns each day wielding the scalpel while the others directed the dissector through guidebooks. I really gained a spiritual gratitude for the woman who had donated her body so I could begin my sojourn of learning to become a physician. It was during this time I wrote my essay "From Parenthood to Physicianhood." In the essay, I wrote about my experiences taking Christy into her surgeries, including the corrective open heart surgery at UCLA. I talked about the calling to become a doctor and my acceptance to UC Davis. I submitted the essay to The Western Journal of Medicine, hoping to have it considered for publication in the monthly human interest section. It was humbling and exciting to hear the reply that it was scheduled to be published. Seeing my first published written work when the issue arrived was unbelievable, and I sent copies to all of my family and friends.

Throughout my first year in medical school, all of my fears I had going in regarding my ability to keep up with the other students were nonexistent. I earned straight As the first and second quarters and missed straight A's in the third quarter by one percentage point in microbiology. I had actually failed the first midterm in the class. This was the first and only test I had ever failed in my life. The lectures leading up to the test were extremely detailed regarding characteristics of each type of bacteria, their gram stain properties, and other minutia. The day prior to the exam, the professor made the statement to focus on the big issues and not to get bogged down in all the details. Well, the exam was all on the minute details, which I had mistakenly avoided to study. After the humiliation of this failure, I resolved to excel on the next two tests and the final in an attempt to recover my grade. I ended up with an 89 percent overall in the course, with an A considered 90 percent and above. All pleading for leniency to the professor went unheeded, as he justified my grade by stating there had to be a cutoff point and if he allowed me slack he would have to give the same to others.

During this quarter, I began to believe that my scholarly success was all due to me, and I began to prioritize grades and school over Susan and my children. When she would try to get me to take the time to do activities with the family, I would tersely state that my studies and school came first. The morning of the second midterm in microbiology, we had a fight about my attitude and priorities. I was so stressed out that I actually slapped her across the face and told her to "Shut the hell up!" Susan began to sob and sat on the floor. This all occurred in front of Christy, who was also crying, and I have regretted the way I acted that morning my entire life. I have never again and never will hit Susan in anger as long as I live.

This last quarter of first year was the lowest point in our marriage, and Susan actually considered leaving me and taking the children back to San Diego. Two events occurred that quickly realigned my priorities and both were distinct acts of God in my life.

BY THE BACK OF THE COLLAR

The first event that would reshape my life occurred after our summer course affectionately known as path camp. The summer quarter was spent in all—day classes and labs designed as an intensive introduction to human pathology, or the study of diseases in people. This was the foundation for our clinical years in third and fourth year, and focused for the first time on abnormal issues in the body rather than normal functions. It was, as billed, the most intense course I would take in medical school. Similar to my first year, I started the course with exceptional performance, and by the week before the final, I was the highest student in the class. Somewhat embarrassed when the professor announced this to the entire class, I was reconsumed by the feeling that it was all about me. I went into the final believing I would ace the hardest course in medical school. Sometimes what we believe and what God has intended for us aren't necessarily aligned. I ended up with a low C grade on the final, and the professor wrote a note on the top of my exam that questioned, "Perplexing. What happened?" My final grade in the course was a B, and for the next week or two I was depressed, grumpy with my family, and equally perplexed by my poor performance. We had a camping trip planned during my two—week break with the destination of Yosemite Valley. Yosemite is by far one of the most spectacular of creations on God's earth. We had a great time hiking, swimming in the Merced River, and enjoying the valley. I still was feeling down about my performance in path camp and was sitting in camp one afternoon, feeling sorry for myself. Suddenly, from the east end of the valley came a tremendous roar that built intensity over five to seven seconds. It sounded like a massive explosion. I looked down toward Half Dome just in time to see a huge dust cloud rising up and over the valley from the base of the monolith. We all jumped on our bikes and rode them down as close as we could get to the granite pile that has accumulated over centuries at the base of the Half Dome face. A new slab that must have weighed many hundreds of tons had fallen from the face and now was lying on top of the pile. In one swift act of nature, God had shown me that he is above all of the other priorities in my life.

The second event occurred at the end of my first quarter of second year. For most of the summer, I had noticed a slight pain in my left ear, which seemed worse when I swallowed food or coughed. While working at one of the student—run clinics during first quarter, I asked the preceptor, a well—respected and student—favored family doctor to look in my ear. I had been waterskiing a lot during the summer and thought I must have some water in my middle ear or even an infection. He said he didn't see anything but maybe I had a swollen lymph node in my neck. He advised me to see an ear, nose, and throat doctor if it didn't clear up within four to six weeks.

In mid January, I made an appointment with a local ENT doctor in Davis; and during the visit, he did a very thorough exam of my ears, mouth, and throat. He put a glove on one hand and put a finger into my throat to feel around. After the exam, he told me he was going to let me recover from all the probing and that he would return soon. After a few minutes, he came back in the room with a hesitant look on his face.

He stated, "Well I know what is causing your ear pain."

I quickly asked if I had an infection, and he said no, that he had found a mass on the base of my tongue. Perplexed, I asked why my ear hurt instead of my tongue and what the mass could be caused by. The ENT doctor explained that 90 percent of unexplained ear pain originates in the mouth and throat and the pain is referred to the ear. He was telling me it could be an infected lymph node or some other cause, but I could tell he was dancing around the issue. I bluntly asked him if it could be cancer; and he replied, "Yes, cancer is also a possibility." He scheduled me to have a biopsy done the next day at the community hospital in Davis.

When I got home after the late afternoon appointment, Susan was home from work and jokingly asked, "Well, are you going to die?"

When I started crying, she knew it was the wrong thing to say. I told her there was a distinct possibility I had cancer and we would find out the next day.

The next morning, we checked in early, and the ENT doctor took me into the OR. After the brief procedure, I was awakening from anesthesia and Susan was next to me.

I groggily asked her if it was cancer, and she replied, "I'm not going to lie to you, Mike, you have a cancerous tumor on the base of your left tongue and you need surgery."

After I recovered fully from the effects of anesthesia, the reality of the diagnosis hit me like a runaway train. I had the typical feelings of denial ("This can't be happening to me"), anger, and then eventually the acceptance that it was occurring and I had to do everything I could to fight the battle and stay alive for my family.

I had reservations about having the surgery performed by the community ENT doctor in Davis. He had been describing how he would need to open my jaw on the left, perform a radical neck dissection, and remove a large portion of the base of my tongue. I wasn't convinced that this type of complex surgery was something he had done a lot. I talked to some of my school professors, and the name Paul Donald kept coming up. Both positive and negative perspectives abounded about this head and neck surgeon I had never met.

My decision was helped by a visit with the chair of the pathology department, Murray Gardner. At the time, Murray was a world—renowned AIDS researcher and a brilliant scientist. I obtained my tissue slides from the biopsy and reviewed them with Dr. Gardner just to verify for myself that some mistake hadn't occurred in the pathology lab that had produced the diagnosis. Looking at the slides under the microscope, it was apparent that unless they had used someone else's tissue for the slides, I was in big trouble. The slides revealed a poorly differentiated squamous cell carcinoma. A lot of blue stain appeared in numerous cells, indicating open and replicating DNA, which is the usual finding for rapidly dividing malignant cells.

Dr. Gardner was aware that I was considering having the treatment done by Dr. Donald, and also knew that I was concerned about Paul's reputation for being a very aggressive surgeon who sometimes performed overly aggressive resections, leaving patients with disfiguring changes to their faces, necks, and upper chests. What I did like about Dr. Donald was also this same aggressive reputation. I had a young family and wife that I wasn't ready to leave, so I wanted every possible treatment that would save my life. I was well reassured when Murray told me that, yes, Paul's reputation was concerning, but if it was his tongue cancer, he wouldn't have a second thought about who would be his surgeon: Paul Donald, MD.

The ENT from Davis had set up a consultation visit with a tumor board that consisted of numerous radiation oncologists, as well as head and neck surgeons. This was held at a community hospital in Sacramento. The consensus of the tumor board was that they could radiate the tumor and eliminate it without any surgery. I knew more than I did before starting medical school but certainly not enough to make a life—altering decision about how this should be treated. Compounding the decision was the fact that Paul Donald had told me that choosing only radiation as the primary treatment would guarantee that I would be dead within a year. The only solution I could rely on was leaving it in God's hands and praying for the answer.

On the Sunday before I was scheduled to go into the hospital for a pre—surgical evaluation called a pan—endoscopy and tumor mapping by Dr. Donald, Susan, the kids, and I all attended mass to pray for God's help in making this decision. Before mass started, I casually looked over to my side, and there, sitting a row behind us, was Dr. Donald. God had given me the answer I so badly needed. To know that the man who held my life in his hands realized that God was the one who held all of our lives in His hands was peacefully reassuring.

On Tuesday, after the study, Dr. Donald came into my hospital room. They were keeping me overnight because I had continued bleeding from the areas around the tumor where he had taken biopsy and mapping samples. He wanted me to be aware that the tumor appeared perilously close to the epiglottis and might actually extend into the tissues of the larynx. He wanted me to consent for a possible laryngectomy, or removal of my vocal chords. While I was hearing this from him, I could only think about how it would be virtually impossible to be a practicing doctor without a normal voice and ability to communicate adequately with patients. I told him I would let him know after I had a chance to discuss it with Susan. When it came time to sign the consent form before surgery, I told him that I didn't want to consent for a laryngectomy and that if the tumor extended into the tissues of the larynx, I would want to be woken up and told so I could prepare myself for losing my voice as I knew it. He reluctantly agreed to this request, and we scheduled my surgery.

Susan drove me to the hospital early in the morning of February 7, 1989. I felt like a lamb being led to slaughter, and she sensed my apprehension. She helped me into my hospital gown and then took my hands and prayed that God would watch over me and guide Dr. Donald's hands as he cut into my neck and throat during the surgery. Lying in the pre—op area, I began reflecting on how I had started to believe that becoming a physician was my doing and my success and had forgotten that without God and a supportive, loving wife, none of what I had done would have been possible. I had strayed so far from the right priorities and this was God's way of turning me back onto the path of humility and gratitude rather than the path of self—righteousness and pride. I was frightened yet felt very peaceful and confident that everything would be all right. When I awoke from surgery, I had a tracheostomy and was unable to speak. I was in the ICU, and my loving wife was by my side. I had to write everything down to communicate, but I still had my larynx intact. Dr. Donald had done an approach and resection that he had never before attempted. He developed it as he was operating on me, visualizing a new way of layering back the epithelium of the epiglottis and removing the tissues in the pre—epiglottic space as well as widely resecting the left base of my tongue. A day or two later, the speech therapist came by and explained to me how I could talk by plugging the trach tube and letting the air flow up and through my vocal chords. I tried multiple times, but the tissues in my mouth and neck were still too swollen to be successful. I had a feeding tube through my right nostril and had to pump a high—calorie liquid diet through it twenty—four hours per day to keep my intake up, which would help heal my surgical sites. I felt so helpless and completely dependent on other people. Every day, Susan would be there, sitting by my side, responding to my written requests for help. As I looked at her, I realized how I had been taking her love and our matrimony for granted and had gotten so askew in my life and my relationship with God. In many ways, what I went through with that bout of cancer was more of a gift than a cross to bear. The physical pain and disabilities would resolve, but unless I got my spiritual priorities straight, becoming a doctor would cost me much more than the money for medical school. This had been my wake—up call and God's way of applying tough love to my hardheadedness.

Every day, all day, I kept trying to speak, but the time was not right. On St. Valentine's Day, February 14, Susan came into my room and I squeakily eked out a high—pitched, "I love you!" It took both of us by surprise, but it was unmistakable. I had said my first words after the surgery.

Recovery was a long, slow process. I was discharged with the naso-gastric tube sutured into my nose for tube feedings until all the swelling in my mouth and oropharynx resolved. Six weeks after surgery, I was just beginning to eat on my own and felt pretty good. My first food was a tuna sandwich that took me almost two hours to eat completely.

The six—week point after surgery was the start of seven weeks of post—operative radiation, and I tolerated the first half well. The side effects of radiation began to manifest when I started the second half of treatment. I began losing my saliva, and it was very painful to eat solids, as my esophagus was extremely inflamed from the treatments. I had taken a leave of absence from school for the second year, as I knew I would be unable to attend classes and study.

During a follow—up visit with Paul Donald, he asked if I had smoked marijuana in the past. I was completely honest with him and told him my history of regular use of marijuana from the age of thirteen until just after David was born, when I was twenty—three. He explained that he had a cohort of about thirteen patients all of whom had used marijuana regularly in their youth and now were being diagnosed with head and neck tumors. These types of cancer typically occurred in the later years with patients who had been long—term tobacco users or alcoholics. It was highly unusual to have it occur in the twenties or early thirties.

After I fully recovered, during my leave of absence, Dr. Donald called me and asked if I would be willing to do an interview with a national news magazine television program that was doing a story on patients with head and neck cancer at a young age and the possible link to smoking marijuana. I had no hesitancy doing this for him since he had essentially saved my life. I interviewed with PM Magazine, the program doing the story. Additionally, the BBC picked up the story and also interviewed me and our children about the implications and possible link to marijuana use. I also did a couple of appearances at high school programs on drug abuse and talked about the experience of losing a large portion of my tongue as well as a disfiguring radical neck dissection. It was the least I could do for Paul and something I had to do for God if my own stupidity in my youth had caused this insult to the sanctity of my body. After all, it is God's body, not mine, and He has just lent it to me to use for a short time.

A professor in physiology whose research area was pulmonary physiology offered me a one year pre—doctoral fellowship working on research projects in his lab since I was going to lose the whole year of school. Every weekday, I went to the Med Sciences building and worked on several ongoing projects with Jerry, the professor, as well as some undergraduate students who volunteered in order to add the experience to their applications as they went through the admission process for medical school.

During the year off, I was primary author on one publication and secondary author on several others, all of which were accepted for publication. Despite losing the year, I was able to salvage some productivity that would bolster my curriculum vitae or CV. This is a summary of a professional person's career, listing their education, training, job positions, research, publications, and lectures. Several of the publications were presented at a scientific meeting in Washington, DC, so Susan and I got a nice trip to our nation's capital as well as a side trip to New York City. This was by far the longest distance that either of us had ever traveled from California. It was overwhelming to visit all of the Smithsonian museums and humbling to stand at the graves of John and Bobby Kennedy in Arlington Cemetery.

Before resuming my second year the following fall, we had multiple opportunities to travel as a family in a used motor home we had purchased. We took trips to Yellowstone, Yosemite again, Kings Canyon, the Oregon coast, and even went to British Columbia and Victoria. We were reinventing our life together as a family, and my priorities were now focused on my loved ones. I left the issue of completing medical school in God's hands and was amazed at how things came together well, without me being self—focused or ignoring my loving wife and children.

I completed the second year and did very well on the national board examinations, despite having virtually no sleep the night before the start of the two—day test. I was nervous, without a doubt, but it was actually our animals that kept me awake all night. Our old dog, Kimba, decided that was the night to dig a hole in the backyard, right under our open bedroom window. We had also gotten Christy a kitten several months before, a black cat we named Pepper. Along with the digging dog, the cat was batting something against our closed bedroom door. When I decided I wasn't going to fall asleep with all this chaos, I got up to see what the cat was doing. She had a mostly dead mouse that she was playing with and must have wanted to show us her great find.

The national board examinations are the major hurdle between the first two years and final two clinical years of medical school. Every student worries about failing the tests, and about eight percent actually do fail. Those two days were the most grueling of my student life, and as is true for every student, I felt like I had failed them. When I got my results a couple of months later, I found I had scored in the ninetieth or higher percentile in every area. This time around, however, I knew it was because of the grace of God and not my own accomplishments. I was on the way to my clinical years of medical school, working with practicing doctors and learning the skills of being a physician. .

"A faithful man shall abound with blessings…"

Proverbs 28:20

"The hairy polyester" wedding of Mike and Susan, April 19, 1975.

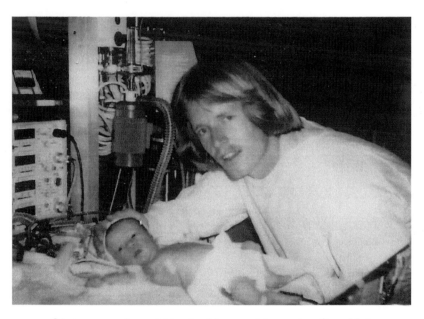

Christy at 2 days old in the Neonatal Intensive Care Unit
prior to her first surgery.

Christy's first baby photo. Notice the dusky blue hue
to her face, lips, and skin.

Christy's beloved pink "blankie" at age 2.

Christy at age 4 showing off her new scar
from open heart surgery at UCLA.

Brother and sister photo of David and Christy, ages 5 and 2.

Christy and fiancé Steve on Kauai, Hawaii.

Newlyweds in Lake Tahoe, July 22, 2006.

Newlywed couple, David and Michelle Carl, October 14, 2006.

Susan and Mike, celebrating our 30th anniversary
on a Panama Canal cruise, 2005

The light of our lives, Noah Michael, Christmas 2010

Christy and her "Heart Hero", Dr. Hillel Laks of UCLA, who performed
her first open heart repair at age four. Photo taken at a conference for
Adult Congenital Heart Patients held in Los Angeles, May, 2011.

STORIES OF
MEDICAL SCHOOL

My first clinical rotation at the beginning of third year was two months of psychiatry. I started it with trepidation. The only person I had even remotely known in my life with mental illness was the woman who lived about four blocks away from my home where I grew up in San Diego. One day, something snapped in her and she took her three young children out onto the front yard and proceeded to carve them up with a butcher knife. By the time a neighbor had heard screaming, she had mortally wounded all three and they were dead on the scene when the emergency crews arrived. This was how I envisioned every patient on the inpatient psych unit. I was enlightened to find that most of them had typical cases of schizophrenia, bipolar disorder, or depression and were in the Psychiatric Unit as more of a threat to their own well being that a danger to others. Many were admitted for medication adjustments, and some even were on the schedule to have electroconvulsive treatments (ECT) to shock them back to a relatively normal psychological state. One of the responsibilities on the rotation was to help the social worker who ran the psychiatric emergency services (PES) program in the ER. Two nights each week, I had to spend the hours of 5:00 p.m. to midnight evaluating patients who came into the ER complaining of hallucinations, depression, or any number of acute psychiatric complaints. The first night on call, I was paged by the medical social worker (MSW) to evaluate a woman who came into the ER complaining of hallucinations and vomiting. I walked into the department, and found the patient lying on a gurney in the hallway, begging for help with her nausea and vomiting and every nurse and doctor ignoring her request. I found one of the ER nurses and asked her for a pan the woman could vomit into instead of all down the front of her gown.

"You can find a basin in the supply room," the nurse told me with a nasty rapid reply.

I got the basin, gave it to the woman, and noticed that she smelled like she had spilled an entire bottle of vodka on herself. Trying to find her chart, I searched the pile where the records of newly registered patients were dropped by the chartroom staff. Not finding the chart, I walked over to the medical records office and gave them the patient's name. The staff person working the counter looked it up in the computer and found it sitting on a pile of recently pulled charts destined to eventually be re—filed. I told her it should have been sent to the ER, and she handed it to me to carry it there myself.

I returned to the hallway where she had been when I had tried to get her some help, and the nurse told me she had been roomed. As I walked toward the room where she had been placed, an older, gruff ER doctor came up to me and tersely asked, "Whose chart do you have there?" When I replied with the woman's name, he fiercely looked me in the eye and told me that I was to never, ever take another chart from the ER, especially when he was looking for it to medically clear the patient. I was taken aback by being treated so rudely by someone I had never met before and accused of taking a chart from the ER.

I shot back at him, "This chart wasn't in the ER! I walked over to the chartroom myself to find it and bring it here. I need to evaluate her for the PES service and need to know her previous history!"

He looked somewhat sheepishly and told me he needed it for just a few minutes and then would leave it on the desk outside her room. This night had been my first run in with an ER doctor and ER nurse and left me with a disappointed feeling for possible future colleagues.

The days in the locked adult inpatient psychiatry unit were nothing if not completely entertaining. There was an Italian twenty—something—year—old young man with supposed depression who seemed to find his way into the rooms and beds of every young female patient on the unit. My suspicion was that he had found three meals a day, a warm environment, and all the sex he could handle. How depressing could that be? One day, my resident and I admitted a young married woman with a history of schizophrenia who was manifesting multiple personalities. As part of her workup to rule out any organic cause of her mental changes, she needed a lumbar puncture, or spinal tap. I had watched the resident perform one a few days earlier on another patient, and he told me it was my turn to perform the procedure.

I asked, "Really?!"

His response was, "The long—standing tradition in medical school in regard to procedures is, 'See one, do one, teach one,' and now you're up for the 'do one' part of it." I introduced myself to the woman as Student Doctor Carl, and asked if she was okay with me doing the lumbar puncture. She said she was, so I went about preparing the tray, positioning her on her side, and prepping her back with Betadine. I put on sterile gloves and draped her back with a sterile cover. I proceeded to inject her with a local anesthetic, followed by inserting the 3.5" spinal needle slowly between her second and third lumbar vertebrae. Slowly advancing the needle, I felt a slight "pop" as the needle tip entered the epidural space. Advancing the needle by one to two millimeters at a time, I pulled the inner trochar, or central piece of the hollow needle, out with each slight push until, suddenly, clear fluid began dripping from the end of the needle. I had just performed my first lumbar puncture successfully. The cerebrospinal fluid was collected in the four plastic sterile tubes that came with the kit and sent off to rule out meningitis or infection with syphilis as the cause of her mental changes. This was also the first time I had performed a significantly invasive procedure in medical school other than doing blood draws on fellow students, and I was proud I was able to do it without the resident having to jump in and complete it for me.

The next rotation after I completed psychiatry was pediatrics. I was assigned to rotate at the Air Force hospital on Travis Air Force Base about 30 miles southwest of Sacramento. I found it interesting to rotate at a different hospital and learned to care for hospitalized pediatric patients. This included putting in tiny IV's, drawing blood on babies, and doing minor procedures such as lumbar punctures on infants and toddlers.

The third year was rounded out with the other mandatory rotations in OB—GYN, internal medicine, and surgery. One of the surgical specialties I rotated on was orthopedics. I really enjoyed the camaraderie with the residents and the mechanical aspect of the specialty. I learned to drill bones, cut bone, and install hardware into joints and long bones. It was very easy, as it made use of my skills as a plumber and used tools in a similar manner. I really thought I might like to go into orthopedics but was concerned because it was a five— to six—year residency. It also required six months of every other night call in the first and second years of the residency. I was so interested, however, that I set up to rotate on an acting internship in the summer of my fourth year. This was going to be done at the UC Davis Medical Center, and I would be working with the spine team.

One of the required rotations during fourth year was a month in the Emergency Department. I was scheduled to do this after my one month AI in orthopedics. I had always been mildly disappointed in potentially becoming an orthopedist, as I would not make use of my training in other specialties. When I rotated through the ER, I found that I had an opportunity to see patients with every possible medical problem, including gynecologic, pediatric, internal medicine, surgery, and orthopedic problems. I began to realize that what I enjoyed the most about orthopedics was diagnosing fractures in the ER and treating acute injuries rather than the surgical aspects of the specialty. A residency in emergency medicine was also only three years, only about half the time of orthopedics. After my health issues and time off in second year, I didn't think doing a six—year residency with so much time away from Susan and the kids would be fair to them.

I also was interested in critical care medicine, so I decided to interview for residency positions in this specialty along with emergency medicine programs. A program that was very interested in me was the pulmonary/critical care fellowship at Scripps Hospital in La Jolla, just north of San Diego on Torrey Pines beach. I would do internal medicine there and then continue into the fellowship at the same institution.

The attraction for going this route was returning to our hometown of San Diego and training at a very prestigious institute. I was conflicted between this opportunity and emergency medicine. The choice was to train at a very prestigious program, go into a respected specialty, and care for patients who were well off and insured. This was compared to emergency medicine, where I would be caring for the marginalized and downtrodden in our society, most of whom were either uninsured or covered by Medi—Cal.

As I entered the hospital, I was overwhelmed by the beauty of the lobby and reception areas. The chief resident toured two of us through the units and floors, and the elegance of every aspect was astounding. This certainly would be a beautiful, well—staffed environment to do my medical training.

THE EYES OF A SAINT

Prior to this visit at Scripps, I had been praying that God would help make my decision obvious. There were so many pros and cons between the two specialties, but my heart was leaning toward emergency medicine. This was because of the variety of cases, the opportunity to make a difference in patients' lives during one of the most frightening times of their existence, the opportunity to help the less fortunate in our society, and the shorter training time to starting practice.

As we entered the Scripps elevator in the lobby, the chief resident was telling me and the other candidate about all of the benefits of training at the hospital. The call rooms were elegant with televisions and complete privacy. The cafeteria served an incredible variety of excellent foods, and the dining room overlooked the beautiful blue Pacific Ocean. We rode the elevator up to the third floor to see the ICUs. Our car stopped on the second floor, and the doors opened for a group of three or four people surrounding an elderly nun in a blue—and—white habit being pushed in a wheelchair. As I looked out of the elevator, my eyes met the piercing blue eyes of Mother Teresa, who nodded to me and waved with two fingers placed up to her forehead and sent in my direction. She was dressed exactly as she always was in every photo I had ever seen of her, and it almost appeared as though a halo surrounded her head. The look on my face had to be one of utter disbelief. My mouth dropped open as the group with Mother Teresa decided to wait for the next car and the doors closed. I looked to the female candidate standing next to me, and we both asked each other, "Was that who I think it was?" The chief resident quickly answered that it was just a nun who was in the hospital and they had lots of religious who received their care at Scripps.

As we got off the elevator and walked onto the critical care floor, I continued to talk with the other candidate, exclaiming that it had to be Mother Teresa. There was just nobody in the world that looked like her. The resident stopped us at the side of a hallway and told us that it was her but they were keeping her admission confidential to avoid a media circus. She had been in Tijuana, Baja California, Mexico visiting her clinic she had recently established there when she suffered a mild heart attack. She was flown by helicopter from the clinic to Scripps and admitted for testing and therapy. She had been on her way to radiology for some x—rays when that elevator door fatefully opened.

I left Scripps with the certainty that I should go into emergency medicine. I had just looked into the eyes of a future saint who had lived her life ministering to the poor, the downtrodden, and the street dwellers of Calcutta. This was an unequivocal sign from God that I should walk in those same footsteps in my choice for medical training. I might never reach the poor of India; but here was an opportunity to minister to the poor of our society, many of whom are homeless, without regular meals, and seeking treatment when medical problems had progressed to a life—threatening point due to lack of insurance or a regular source of medical care. That afternoon, I called and cancelled two other visits scheduled to look at critical care programs and focused my efforts on emergency medicine.

EVOLUTION OF AN ER DOCTOR

During my third and fourth year of medical school, I had earned straight A's on all of my clinical rotations and had been elected to the Alpha Omega Alpha, or AOA, medical honor society at the end of third year. This was a tremendous recognition and carried a lot of weight as residency programs evaluated me for acceptance. AOA membership was given to those students who were felt to be examples of future excellence in medicine, and there were eight students elected in third year with eight more being elected halfway through fourth year. I was humbled and grateful when I received the call I was now an AOA member in my third year of school.

Because of my clinical performance, I really had my choice of where I wanted to complete residency. I knew we wanted to stay in California, so, like acceptance to medical school, I only interviewed at California programs. The two top programs in emergency medicine at that time were Harbor UCLA and Fresno, one of the oldest residency programs in emergency medicine in the country. It was started just a few years after the Cincinnati program, the first. I interviewed at Stanford, UC Davis, UC San Diego, UC Irvine, and Fresno. I didn't want my family living in Los Angeles, so Harbor UCLA was off the table as a choice.

My preference was the Fresno program. It was well established with a strong reputation in emergency medicine around the country. The downside was that it is a four—year program and that fourth year equated to giving up about $100,000 in starting salary as a staff physician. We drove down to look at the area and decided that if we matched at Fresno, we would look to buy a house in Clovis, a bedroom community just north of the city. Susan and the kids didn't want to leave Davis, however. David and Christy were young teens, and uprooting them again to move to a new area would be rough. Susan had started back to undergraduate studies part—time at UC Davis and wanted to finish her bachelor's degree there. She was majoring in applied behavioral science, which was a unique study and allowed her to custom make her own focus of the degree. She would not be able to finish her degree at any other place. Therefore, the decision was made to rank the UC Davis Medical Center EM program as my first choice. San Diego would be number two since it would be a return home and we still owned our house there.

The Davis program in emergency medicine had only started two years prior to my applying, so it was an unproven training program in that regard. I had some worries about the quality of training I would receive, but this was alleviated somewhat when I found out that 35 percent of the emergency department time was spent at Kaiser Permanente, South Sacramento. I had met the Kaiser attending physicians during the interview process and found out that almost all of them were former chief residents at their residency programs. Two had trained at Denver General Hospital and two at Fresno's Valley Medical Center, arguably the number one and two programs in the country. The others trained at various other programs around the country, giving the emergency medicine group a well—rounded complement of experience. I felt that this was where the majority of my community emergency medicine training would come from, with the UC Davis Medical Center providing more than adequate trauma training along with critically ill patient management skills.

MATCH DAY

Match Day is an interesting phenomenon. It occurs in mid March of the fourth year, and all residents have submitted several weeks prior to the day a list of programs for the area of training they are pursuing. The day before Match Day, the deans of the medical schools are notified of any students who didn't match to one of their choices on their list. A frantic phone call session starts, with the deans calling programs that didn't fill up and trying to arrange a spot for the unmatched students. Most students end up somewhere, but it might not have been near the top or even on their list at all. On Match Day, all fourth—year students meet in a reception atmosphere, usually with some type of food and drink, and they are handed their match results in an envelope. I felt fairly confident that I would match at UC Davis Medical Center, but there was always the possibility that higher—recruited students could fill the program before me. I tentatively opened the envelope and was relieved that there were no surprises and I had, in fact, gotten a position in the emergency medicine residency at UC Davis. One of my classmates, who also had chosen emergency medicine, matched at Davis also. Kurt, the classmate, had rotated in fourth year with me on neurosurgery. Neurology is a mandatory rotation in the fourth year of medical school, and 99 percent of the students pick Neurology as their rotation. Neurosurgery can be taken as an alternative to Neurology. It is viewed as much more grueling, so very few students pick it for their rotation unless they are considering General Surgery or Neurosurgery as their residency choice. Kurt and I had talked about it, and we both thought neurosurgery made more sense for an emergency physician since head injured patients or someone with a cerebral hemorrhage would come to the ER for their initial evaluation and stabilization.

Neurosurgery was quite an interesting experience for Kurt and me. Neurosurgeons tend to be grumpy and argumentative with each other more times than not. I once asked the chief resident why this was the case, and he replied that if you lived with six other residents for seven years, spending more time with them than a spouse or significant other, you'd be grumpy, too. It was an invaluable experience, however. I had numerous opportunities to assist with brain surgery, drill holes in skulls to place ventriculostomies and pressure monitoring equipment in the brain, and to assist on spinal procedures. Orthopedists and neurosurgeons both operate on the spine, overlapping on the simpler procedures such as fusions and diskectomies. The complicated nerve and tumor surgeries are done exclusively by the neurosurgeons.

RESIDENCY IN EMERGENCY MEDICINE

When Kurt and I found out we were both entering the third class for EM at Davis, we were excited that we might have a chance to work together again in the future. This happens, however, much more infrequently, as the Emergency Medicine (EM) residents are usually paired with residents from internal medicine or family practice. We never crossed paths on rotations, so the only time we saw each other was during our Tuesday morning academic forum. This was a half day of lectures and presentations, and all residents were excused from their assigned rotations to attend. Our fellow first—year residents were a wide cross section of cultures and medical schools attended. There were two women and six men, as most female graduates of medical school chose other areas than emergency medicine in 1992. That has changed dramatically in the past two decades, and most residency classes are now more women than men.

My first four months were spent at Kaiser, South Sacramento, with the first rotation being in the anesthesia department learning to intubate patients as they are prepared for surgery. Many emergency patients come into the ER with altered levels of consciousness and require protection of their airway, or might be having severe breathing distress and require being placed on a ventilator. This is where learning to place a tube into their trachea is absolutely the first basic skill ER doctors need to acquire. Not to mention the fact that in the scheme of critical care or trauma, the algorithm to help you remember the order of events is the ABCs: airway, breathing, circulation, and so on.

The next three months I spent working on the internal medicine service, also at Kaiser South. I took care of a wide variety of very sick patients and managed many in the ICU. The cultural and religious diversity at this hospital made for a lot of learning on my part. I particularly remember a young woman who arrived in the ER comatose and completely unresponsive. She was of Pakistani heritage and had three or four children ranging in age from three to fourteen years old. The ER doctor had performed a CT scan of her head and found that she had suffered a massive hemorrhage in her brainstem and would not survive such an event. We were admitting her to discuss organ donation with the husband and family. When I arrived in the ER to evaluate and admit her to the ICU, she had a very familiar glaze to her eyes that I had seen during medical school in patients who were near death or had just died. Her pupils were fixed and dilated, and she had no reflexes or response to painful stimulation.

It took a very tense two days to convince her husband that she had no chance of surviving the bleed, she was brain dead by all of our testing, and the best outcome would be to use her organs to give life to others. During these two days, her vital signs were tenuous due to sodium loss typically seen in dying brain injury patients. The organ donation agency was assisting with managing the clinical aspects of keeping the patient's body alive long enough to recover her organs. Her husband finally agreed to the donation but requested that I tell the children we were taking their mother into surgery in an attempt to save her life and that she might likely die from the surgery. I had a difficult time accepting the fact that the husband was asking me to lie to his children, but I knew the reality that the greater good would be the outcome if her organs were donated. I asked God to give me strength and help me find the right words to explain the plan to the children. I honored the father's wish and told them we were making a last—ditch attempt to save her life but that she most likely would die in the operating room. I then talked to them about how their mother had a chance to make this terrible situation a little more acceptable by donating her organs to other people facing death if their medical teams weren't able to find them a heart, lung, kidney, or liver transplant in time. There were many, many tears as we prepared to take the woman's body to the OR, but the family was able to say good—bye, and the husband knew in his heart he was making the right decision. All of the organs were recovered, viable, and transplanted within twelve hours in numerous other hospitals around Sacramento. God had helped us find an acceptable end to the life of this beautiful Pakistani wife and mother after such a tragic event in her brain.

It seemed that for a community hospital, there were an inordinate amount of critically ill patients. As an intern on the medicine wards, it was my duty to respond to all deaths and pronounce the patient. One night, I got a page that an elderly woman had died on the third floor and I needed to complete the pronouncement and the death certificate. I went up the elevator from the call room and walked in on a seventy-ish— year—old man holding the woman's hand and silent tears flowing down his cheeks. I placed my hand on his shoulder and softly murmured that I was Dr. Carl, the on—call hospital doctor.

Without even turning to face me, he replied, "Forty—five years. For forty—five years, we were at each other's side, and now she's gone. What am I going to do now?" he queried, more to God than to me. I respectfully listened for breathing and heart sounds, finding none. I opened her eyes to check for light and corneal reflexes, her eyes almost a mirror image of those of the Pakistani woman. I told her husband I would complete the death certificate and asked if he had any questions for me.

"Why does it go by so fast?" he asked me, this time looking straight into my face with his red—rimmed eyes. I had no response that I could even begin to muster. I asked him if I could bless her body with a sign of the cross on the forehead and a silent prayer. He was happy to have me do it, and this became my action with every person in my career that I was fortunate enough to be with when they passed over to the other side of life.

Many times during residency training and later during my career, I have fought to hold back my own tears in these times of loss of life and family tragedy. I have usually been successful, being able to be professional and yet empathetic when talking with families about a loved one's critical condition or death. I would usually go home and break down while telling Susan about the experience. This seemed to be a good catharsis for me and enabled me to go back on duty the next day, ready to face whatever came. There are three distinct times I remember not being able to suppress my emotions and losing it in front of families or patients. The first was a trauma activation at UC Davis when I was the second—year resident on the trauma rotation. The paramedics brought in a three—year—old boy who had fallen off his family's boat while it was moving. He sat upright on the gurney, holding a blanket and teddy bear the EMS crew had given him. He looked every bit the part of a normal, cute little boy, except one aspect. His right leg had been severed just above the knee when the propeller hit him. There was no crying, no fussing; just the look of a cute, little, blond—haired angel ready for whatever would come next. The thigh had been bandaged on scene, and dive crews were searching the lake bottom to attempt to find the rest of the leg in case it could be reattached. I was overcome by the sight and had to leave the trauma room to pull myself together. I was imagining how I would feel if he was my son and was facing the rest of his life with a prosthetic leg.

The second event where I lost my emotional control happened also in the UC Davis ER, during board rounds and change of shift. The paramedics had transported an African American man into the ER after he had been detained by police at an apartment building where shots were reportedly fired. As they brought the chiseled—bodied, shirtless black man into the internal triage area, I noticed numerous monochromatic tattoos on his arms, neck, and upper chest, and back. These tattoos are usually attained only in prison, and they are one color, the color of the writing pen that was drained for the ink used to make the tattoos. They were gang insignia, either from pre—prison gangs or prison gangs in which he was a member. He was assigned a room in area three and taken there by the paramedics. The attending physicians who were standing around, taking part in the sign—out rounds, began making derogatory comments about not wanting to be around when the gang members came in to finish him off, or wondering who had gotten the worst of the skirmish, or betting whether or not he was packing a hidden weapon. When board rounds had finished, I picked up a chart to see a patient, and it was the same man. I walked into his room, and he was standing up at the side of the bed.

"I just want to leave," he said after putting on a hospital gown.

I noticed he was holding his abdomen as though he were in pain. I couldn't see any blood soaking through his gown or pants, but he was obviously very uncomfortable. I told him my name and asked if he would let me examine him before he left the ER.

"Why do you even care about me?" he asked me. "I'm just a dumb nigger who has done a lot of bad things in my life. I just got out of prison for some of those things, and as far as I know, they could have been to your family."

I tried to reassure him that he hadn't hurt me or my family and that I cared about him as a fellow human being. I sat on the edge of the gurney and invited him to do the same. As I looked at his face and his prison tattoos, I suddenly noticed tears welling in his eyes.

"Man, when they let me out yesterday, all I wanted to do was to see my daughter who was born when I was in there and try to make a normal life for her. I put my life together in the pen. I got baptized and became a born—again Christian. But when all you got to come back to is the same 'hood, the same gangsters who want you to smoke crack with them and commit crimes, there is no escape no matter how much you want it."

It was heart wrenching to see this toughened man who had nothing but bad breaks or no breaks at all in life sitting next to me with tears running down his cheeks.

"Please just forget about me and let me go back to where I came from so you can take care of patients who really need your help. There's no helping me, and it's just a matter of time before I'm dead from a bullet."

As I tried to talk him into a quick exam and some pain medication, I could see that I wasn't going to convince him to stay. So I reluctantly told him I needed him to sign a paper that said he was leaving AMA, or against medical advice.

"I'll sign it if you'll let me get out of here," he responded.

I walked up front to the Clerk's desk and had her stamp up an AMA form. When I walked back into the pulled curtain, the gurney was empty. He had grabbed a blanket I had given him, presumably to keep warm as he walked the streets. He had left the ER before I even got to offer him a taxi ride back home. All I could do was sit on the end of the gurney and let the tears flow. I cried with emotional pain for the lack of equality in our country, despite all of our progress with civil rights. I cried for what this poor Christian man was facing in his environment, and the racism that still permeates our society, even within ER doctors who were getting a profiling laugh at the expense of this man who just wanted a real life for his daughter and himself. The attending, a very nice woman internist, saw me sitting there and asked if I was all right. I told her no and that I needed to take some time to pull myself together. She said to take all the time I needed, so I walked in the cool night air over to the house staff building where all the call rooms were located. I grabbed an empty room, locked the door, and lay on the hard bed. I tried to understand how this man had affected me so, and then I realized that God had brought us together to help each other understand the disparity between our lives. I prayed for him for several minutes, asking God to lead him to peace and help him escape the lock of the ghetto, the only life other than prison that he had ever known. Here was a man who was probably right. He had done so many bad things in his life, some of which could have been targeted at my family or friends. He had spent numerous years in the hellhole of prison, paying for his crimes. He had an inordinately higher risk of dying from violence than me or any of the people in my life. Yet, he still had the love for his child and God, and the capacity to shed tears of sadness for his plight. I felt a sense of hope and peace fill me, and I prayed that he might feel the same after our interaction together there in bed thirty—five of the ER.

The last time I cried openly in the ER was as an attending physician in my job at Kaiser Permanente, South Sacramento. After I completed residency, I had the choice of a faculty position at UC Davis Medical Center or the staff position at Kaiser. Since medicine was my second career, I was starting much later than usual, finishing residency at the age of forty—one. Retirement benefits were definitely a factor as I chose between the two offers. I could maximize my retirement working twenty years with Kaiser Permanente, which would put me at sixty—one. The UC Davis position could not match the Kaiser benefit package. Since I had been self—employed leading up to medicine, I had very little savings left from my plumbing career after paying for my education and supporting my family for five years. So it was quite an easy decision based on my needs.

Several years into my career, I was working a day shift at the Kaiser ER when a call came in from paramedics about an unresponsive two—month—old baby. I called the pediatrician on call, a very nice woman I knew from residency training, and we both met the EMS crew as they rolled into the ER. The mother was sitting on the gurney, holding the infant in her arms and crying. One of the paramedics pulled me aside and told me that the baby was dead and had never shown any vital signs after their arrival. They didn't have the heart to tell this to the mother. Vicki, the pediatrician, and I went to the mother and asked what had happened. The mother worked night shifts, and her husband cared for the baby while she was at work. She would sleep for a few hours and then care for her baby daughter during the day as her husband worked his job. That morning, she had lain on the couch, holding the baby on her chest. Usually, she would do this to get the baby asleep and then try to sleep herself. This particular morning, she was very tired as she lay with the baby on her. The mother fell asleep, and when she awakened, she had rolled on top of the baby, pinning it between her body and the back of the couch. The baby was unresponsive, so she called 911. Vicki began talking to the mother as I listened for any signs of life. As the paramedics had found, there was no heartbeat and no respiratory effort. The baby was cold and blue. The mother had inadvertently killed her own baby. Both of us sensitively told this to the mother, and we both started crying for the mother's pain. We stood there, both of us with arms wrapped around the mother, trying, ineffectively, to tell her it was an accident and wasn't her fault. After twenty minutes, or so, the social worker was able to convince the mother to let us take the baby to the morgue and helped the mother make calls to family and arrangements for the baby's body. It was so hard to see the pain this mother felt and the guilt overwhelming her for what had been just a tragic accident. We always ask ourselves, during times like these, how can a loving, benevolent God allow such tragedy and loss of life to occur to good people and families? I have learned through the years that it really comes down to free will. God allows us to live our lives, making choices as we do so, and living with those choices we make. We don't even have to choose to believe in God at all if we don't want to know Him. If God revealed all of His power and presence to each and every one of us in our lives, there would be no free will. We would have no choice but to believe in Him and follow Him regardless of our desires and wants. Losses such as the death of this innocent baby hurt profoundly at the time we are in the situation, but our time and life on earth is but a blink of the eye in terms of eternity. Death is just the beginning.

It has been such a humbling honor and a rewarding career as an emergency physician to be able to take care of patients of all ages and at all stages of life and death. While many patients' lives are saved by our work in the ER, sometimes we aren't able to do anything to help them survive. Other times, we can miss critical problems or make mistakes and it costs a patient their life. As a second—year resident, I moonlighted at several small hospitals after I obtained my medical license. A physician's license requires only the first year, or internship, for training. After the completion of internship, a doctor can practice as a generalist and even start his or her own clinic. Very few do, however, as most group practices and hospitals require completed residency training in some area of specialty.

We had run through the majority of our savings during the five years spent as a medical student, so I needed to augment my small salary of $32,000 per year to support a family of four. There was a small, two—bed ER in the Central Valley town of Patterson. I could make the drive from our house in Davis in just less than two hours and work twenty—four—hour shifts during an off weekend. I remember one night when an ambulance brought in an older man in cardiac arrest and under CPR. I checked his endotracheal tube and verified the paramedics had successfully intubated him. He was being ventilated with a bag—valve—mask by one of the paramedics, and we put him on a monitor right away. He was still in ventricular fibrillation, where the all—important lower chambers of the heart were "quivering" or fibrillating rather than rhythmically pumping blood into the lungs and body. I called for the paddles and defibrillated him or shocked his heart to try to restore a regular rhythm. After the second attempt, he had a wide, regular pattern on the monitor, and I could feel faint pulses with each beat. Having only run three or four codes in my young medical career, I wasn't fine—tuned in all the nuances of what medications to give and when to give them. I followed the advanced life support or ALS protocols and ordered a dose of intravenous Lidocaine, thinking we had shocked him into ventricular tachycardia. Immediately after the nurse administered the IV Lidocaine, the rhythm slowed on the monitor and steadily disappeared. Checking his pulse, there was none, and I called for the paramedic to resume CPR. Despite numerous rounds of other medications and defibrillation attempts, I ended up pronouncing the patient dead and comforting the wife and adult son who had arrived shortly after the ambulance. They thanked me for my efforts and left arm in arm to drive home. Several weeks later, during didactic lectures, I learned about idioventricular rhythm (IVR), an intermediate response to defibrillation that can sustain the patient while more definitive treatment occurs. The one drug you don't want to administer during this rhythm is Lidocaine, which will usually stop the rhythm rather than helping it. Although he probably wouldn't have survived such an insult to his heart, and only 1 percent of CPR recipients live to leave the hospital, my lack of knowledge regarding IVR probably cost this man any chance he had of survival. I asked God to forgive me for this mistake and knew I would never repeat such a critical mistake again.

Another humbling case occurred a few years after starting at Kaiser. An elderly, thin man came to the ER complaining of ongoing episodes of intermittent chest pain. This had been going on for the prior year, and the gentleman had been just recently evaluated in the cardiology department with an EKG, exam, and a Persantine—Thallium test. He was unable to walk for a sustained period on a treadmill, so this P—Thal, as it is called by the medical personnel, was performed instead to evaluate for cardiac disease. Persantine is a drug that , dilates the coronary arteries and mimics the heart's response to exercise. Thallium is injected into a vein and circulates throughout the body. It is preferentially taken into muscle, especially recently active muscle, such as the heart, after beating at a high rate. The heart is then scanned and areas of uptake in the heart are evaluated. If one or another area has less uptake of Thallium, it is indicative of damaged or scarred muscle, such as in the case of a past or recent heart attack.

The P—Thal in this patient was completely normal and had just been completed two weeks prior to his ER visit. Just to be safe, I called the cardiologist who had evaluated him during the consultation and discussed the current visit with him. He remembered the patient very well and asked what his pain was like during the current visit. I explained that it was very atypical for angina or MI feeling like a sharp jab in his left side and occurring with no associated symptoms. The patient described it as being relieved when he would lie on his left side for a few minutes. He had felt it today during his working as a waiter in a downtown restaurant and lay down on a back room cot. After a few minutes, the pain resolved and he was able to return to working his lunchtime shift. After completing the shift, he came in to the ER just to be sure. The cardiologist recounted how the studies done recently were all normal and there was no evidence of ischemic heart disease in this patient. In fact, during the actual P—Thal, the patient had an episode of the pain and had no changes on his monitor or a repeat EKG. This had been directly witnessed by the cardiologist, and he was completely satisfied the patient had no heart disease.

I had noticed during my history taking and exam of the patient that he seemed extremely nervous. He was continually straightening his black work slacks and brushing off small crumbs of bread or food from the restaurant job, even long after every piece of debris was gone. I began to believe the nice man might have either a generalized anxiety disorder or even obsessive—compulsive disorder. I offered him a low dose of Valium while waiting for his laboratory results, and he readily accepted it. When I re—evaluated him after all his labs returned completely normal, he was feeling much better and all discomfort had resolved. I set up an evaluation for the next day with a social worker in psychology and discharged him home with his wife and minister, both of whom arrived together shortly after the patient. I explained to them what the cardiologist had told me and my working diagnosis of anxiety disorder. They were happy I was able to get to the bottom of his episodes and offer him some medication for relief. They left around 3:00 p.m., and I continued a very busy shift that was scheduled to end at midnight. Shortly before the end of my shift, the department chief, who was working with me, came and got me from another patient's side.

He told me, "The chest pain patient you saw earlier today just arrived by ambulance and is under CPR."

Stunned, I couldn't remember seeing any chest pain patients during the shift, and then it dawned on me it was the nice elderly gentleman with the anxious manner. My chief said he would continue managing the patient and even talk to the family for me if I wanted.

"No," I replied. "I need to talk with them and find out what happened."

I walked into our triage room where the wife, minister, adult son, and some other supporters from their church were gathered.

"What happened?" I queried the group.

The minister explained that they had all been at a church service that evening and then returned to his house for some dessert and socializing. The patient began having his typical episode, and the minister helped him lie down on a bed for a few minutes. He left the patient alone and then came back to check on how he was doing. He was unresponsive and had no pulse, so they started CPR and called 911.

I excused myself to check on the patient, knowing that his likelihood of surviving was nil. My chief confirmed they had called the code and the patient had expired. I went back into the room with the family and friends and told them how sorry I was that he had died. I couldn't give them any explanation of what happened and only could say that if I could do it over again, I would have asked the cardiologist to admit the patient for further work—up, even though there was no supportive reason for doing this based on his symptoms and prior tests. I expressed again, how deeply sorry I was that he had died just hours after being evaluated in the ER. No autopsy was requested by the family, so I never learned the cause of his unexpected death.

Knowing that I had done the right things, I couldn't find anything I could have done to improve the outcome. I expected a malpractice claim to be filed in the future, but none was ever sought by the family. Perhaps their faith in God led them to believe it was his time and nothing was going to change that fact.

DOCTORS AREN'T PERFECT

Doctors aren't perfect and never will be. All we can do is take care of patients the best we can and pray we make the right decisions where life and death are concerned. Technology has advanced greatly over the past few decades and, for the most part, has benefited patients. Sometimes, however, technology can hurt our patients when we rely too heavily on it for answers. Instead of trusting our intuition and physical examination skills or the intuition of the patients for knowing what might be wrong with them, we look to machines and technology to give us the diagnosis. And sometimes we keep patients alive much longer than they wanted to or should have continued to go on living. Part of that comes from families not knowing when to give up trying and also from doctors not being willing to give up the effort.

The one and only malpractice claim made against me in my career was from a devastating case where I relied too much on technology and not enough on my intuition and that of the patient. In the mid 1990s, ultrasound use by emergency physicians was expanding rapidly. We would examine patients with machines right at the bedside and save paging an ultrasound technician to come into the ER in the middle of the night. Our group was on the forefront of this new technique, and several of us published studies looking at the reliability of bedside ultrasound by ER physicians compared with technicians taking still images with a later reading by a radiologist. It found that emergency physicians could learn to perform excellent exams with very little variability between what we were imaging and what could be done by a technician. We rapidly learned to image gallbladders, livers, pregnancies, and color Doppler studies of the legs to evaluate for deep venous thrombi. It was one such study while I was working an overnight shift alone that led to a tragic outcome for one of my patients.

The patient was a very heavy, morbidly obese woman who was actually a Kaiser employee in one of our clinics. She came into the ER late that night, along with her daughter, because she had been having some swelling and pain in her right calf for several days. I examined her legs and thighs very closely for swelling, including measuring her calf circumferences on each side for comparison. There was no significant difference in size, although both were very large with numerous varicose veins. I found no areas of redness but did note one varicose vein on the right calf that was tender when I pressed on it. I brought in the ultrasound machine to examine her deep veins on the legs and followed our protocol developed for studies by our ER group. It was a difficult study, due to her size, but I was able to visualize the deep veins of her knees as well as the upper thigh and found no evidence of clots or blockage. I attributed her pain to the inflamed varicose vein and sent her home with a plan of warm compresses, elevation, and return for repeat ultrasound if the swelling or pain increased. I didn't see any indication to anticoagulate her without any evidence of DVT but still felt uneasy about her diagnosis. She too was concerned that her leg pain and swelling could be coming from an inflamed varicose vein.

The next evening, I came in for a second night shift, and the off—going day physician told me Betty had come back that morning via ambulance under CPR. She had gone to church that Sunday morning and, while in the service, began having severe shortness of breath with extreme distress. Paramedics were called and found her in cardiac arrest when they arrived at the church and brought her in Code 3, which is lights and sirens, to the ER. All attempts to resuscitate her were in vain, and she died that morning in the department where I had just seen her less than twelve hours earlier.

I was devastated by the news, and the ordeal was made harder as e—mails were sent out to all staff talking about the untimely death of one of our longtime employees. I kept running over the case in my mind, wondering what I could have done differently that might have changed the outcome. Should I have asked the ultrasound technician to come in to the department, even though I felt confident in my ultrasound skills? Should I have asked the internist on call to admit the patient without any indication for admission? Should I have anti—coagulated the patient for a follow—up ultrasound in a few days? None of these actions, most likely, would have made any difference in the outcome. The only way I could explain it was that she had developed a DVT in her leg that had moved into her vena cava in the abdomen, where it lodged until the fateful movement into her lungs to become a saddle embolus. This is a blood clot that sits at the branch of the two main pulmonary arteries and blocks all blood flow to the lungs, causing rapid death. A high number of people at risk for blood clots die this way, and the cause is never discovered. Unless an autopsy is performed, the fact that they had a saddle embolism is never identified. In this case, an autopsy was done, and this confirmed the cause of death as such. In the situation I visualized, the leg ultrasound would be negative for DVT, but the lethal clot would still be present, not visible to ultrasound.

The case became a wrongful death action against me personally as well as Kaiser. The organization mandates binding arbitration in all such cases, so a hearing was set up before a retired judge to arbitrate the claim.

It was an emotionally difficult three or four days of testimony about the case, with the patient's husband and daughter in attendance. I could tell the daughter, who was in her mid twenties, was having a difficult time with the whole process. She broke into quiet tears during her testimony of what she had witnessed during my care of her mother. During a break in her session, she, her father, and the plaintiff attorney were standing in lobby of the building where the arbitration was being conducted. I felt so moved by the tears of Betty's daughter that I had to talk with her about the whole situation.

I walked up to her and told her quietly, "I know how hard all of this is on you, and I want you to know how sorry I am your mother died. If I could change the outcome, I would in a heartbeat. I don't want you to have any misgivings about your father bringing a wrongful death claim against me. I understand his feelings, and this action is part of being a doctor. No matter what the judge decides, I'm okay with it."

She wrapped her arms around me and hugged me, saying between tears, "Thank you for saying that."

The arbitration judge found in my favor, ruling that I had met all standards of care and there was no negligence on my part. That, however, didn't change the fact that a co—worker, a wife, a mother, and a future grandmother had died under my care.

It took me a long time to get over the patient's death, and I am probably still not completely over it. You carry cases like this with you for the rest of your life and hope that you learn something from them and don't repeat whatever mistakes you make. Being an emergency doctor carries an inherent risk for such outcomes because you are treating patients with potentially critical illnesses or injuries. I can only hope that in the end, I helped a lot more people than I inadvertently harmed and that I can always say I did the best I could in the given situation.

THE MIRACLE OF MARY

For the past fifteen years or so, Susan and I have been intermittently taking part as sponsors in the Rite of Christian Initiation for Adults (RCIA) program at our Davis parish of Saint James. Only a few times have we been unable to sponsor candidates entering the Catholic Church, and this has usually been when we were planning a vacation during the term of the program. Every year, we say we want to take a break and don't sign up; but the team usually calls us requesting our sponsorship of someone who is older or in special need of support, and we just can't turn them down.

A few years ago, we were sponsoring a couple during the program, and it was the weekend of the Rite of Election. This is a large gathering of all of the RCIA programs from every parish in the diocese and comprises around two thousand candidates, sponsors, and team members. The rite occurs at the Cathedral of the Blessed Sacrament in Sacramento and is led by the bishop of the diocese.

That year, before the rite, I had a foreboding sense that my skills as an emergency physician were going to be required at some point during the night. The bishop had been ill for several months and was awaiting a liver transplant. I hoped and prayed that something wasn't going to happen to him during the rite. He seemed in good spirits and completed the ceremony with no problems, so I put the foreboding sense out of my mind.

Every year, the St. James RCIA team sets up a dinner after the Rite of Election. It is usually held at the Old Spaghetti Factory in downtown Sacramento. This was our destination after the rite was concluded that night. We arrived with about twenty—five members of our group attending, and the restaurant split us into two large rooms. We each ordered and paid for our own meals, and Susan and I were ready to leave for home, as it had been a long night. As we gathered our coats and began leaving the room we had been in, a member of the RCIA team, Jean, came running up to me. Jean shouted, "Mike, come quick! Something is really wrong with Mary!" I ran into the other room to find Mary, an elderly woman who was a member of the RCIA team, lying on the floor of the restaurant and her husband, Vic, hovering over her, calling her name. Vic and Mary were longtime members of St. James's Church but had recently moved to a retirement community in Lincoln, a city east of Sacramento. Ironically, it is the same community where my parents moved to from San Diego in 2001. They now attended the same Catholic Church as my mom and dad and developed a friendship with them. Mary was helping out with RCIA at their old parish of St. James and sponsoring a candidate.

When I got to Mary's side, she was unresponsive to Vic shaking her shoulder, so I felt for a carotid pulse and found none. I asked Vic if she had choked; and he said no, that she just slumped over in her seat long after they had finished eating. I then told Vic that I wasn't feeling a pulse and that we had to start CPR. I performed a precordial thump with my balled—up fist. This forceful blow to the mid chest actually generates about 25 to 30 joules of energy to the heart and sometimes can be enough to defibrillate it back to a normal rhythm. I re—examined her carotid and, not feeling a pulse, started chest compressions. I had Vic provide a rescue breath via mouth—to—mouth every fifteen compressions, but we weren't getting any response. I was begging God not to let her die under my care, thinking how awful it would be for the entire group to witness it and lose Mary altogether.

That made me briefly think about the group around us, and I realized how it was stone silent in the entire room. I quickly took a glance up and saw a large ring of RCIA members, other restaurant patrons, and even the wait staff holding hands and praying through tear—filled eyes. I stopped long enough for Vic to deliver another rescue breath. As I started to resume compressions, I felt Mary's chest rise spontaneously, and she slowly opened her eyes. By then, the paramedics were arriving, summoned by the 911 called placed by the manager.

Mary looked at me and asked, "What happened? What's going on?"

I told her she had collapsed and lost her pulse and I had been doing CPR on her for a couple of minutes. "I had Vic give you rescue breaths," I told her, "as he didn't want me kissing you."

I gave the rundown to the paramedics of all that had occurred, and then Susan and I followed them to the hospital nearby the restaurant. I wanted to speak directly to the doctor on duty and emphasize that this was not a simple case of fainting but that Mary had been completely pulseless when I got to her side. He did the right thing and had her admitted to the hospital for observation and further testing. Outside, in the ambulance bay, the paramedics were cleaning their rig, getting ready for another call. When they saw me and Susan leave the ER, one of them came over to talk about the case.

After I told him the circumstances of what had happened, he told me, "Man, Doc. You're a hero. I want you by my side if I ever go down like that." I answered back that it wasn't about me but it was the Holy Spirit and all the prayers of the entire restaurant that saved Mary. She was transferred to my hospital, as she was a Kaiser member, and underwent a very thorough evaluation. She went home in a couple of days after everything showed a normal heart and no evidence of a heart attack.

The next week, Mary was at the RCIA meeting and kept thanking me and praising me for saving her life. I told her I appreciated her words but that it was the Holy Spirit who saved her life with the massive prayer circle in that room where she collapsed. This event was etched into the memories of every person who witnessed it, and many of them said it had led them to a deeper faith and relationship with God. Mary continues to do well, and a year after her collapse, she returned the favor of prayers for my mother when she was diagnosed with cancer.

OUR PARENTS' CHALLENGES

My mother was a cigarette smoker from her late teens up until the mid 1990s. I never worried about her smoking until I was in junior high school in the late 1960s and the campaign to decrease smoking took off. Scientists had found direct correlation between regular smoking and diseases such as high blood pressure; stroke; and several types of cancer, with lung cancer being the big one. In school, we had regular programs and movies showing the ills of smoking and the effects on the human body as well as programs outing the tobacco companies for their covering up clear data associating cigarette smoke, both direct and secondhand, with a much higher lifetime risk of these diseases. My mom's father had died of tobacco—related lung cancer, and I began to beg her to quit smoking. When Christy was born with her congenital heart defect, her physicians advised that we keep her away from cigarette smoke. This was finally the impetus for my mom to decrease her smoking or at least limit it to when our family wasn't visiting at the house.

After we moved up to Northern California for medical school, our visits to San Diego and visits with both of our sets of parents were limited to the holidays and maybe a week or so in the summer. I was happy to see that my mom had given up smoking completely and kept a water—filled jar of old cigarette butts on the kitchen counter as her motivation. Anytime she felt like she wanted a cigarette, she would open the jar and take a deep smell of the caustic mess in the jar, and that would quickly stifle the urge to light one up.

Susan's father, on the other hand, continued being a daily chain smoker and would move to smoking outside if we were visiting with the kids. If he wasn't going to try to save himself, at least he was willing to protect our children, Christy in particular.

After the third year and before I started my final, fourth year of medical school, we were in San Diego visiting everyone when Susan's father, Bill, told us about a right shoulder bursitis that had been bothering him for several weeks. He saw his primary doctor, who ordered shoulder x—rays as well as chest films to evaluate the pain. Everything came back negative, so he was prescribed some anti—inflammatory medications and physical therapy. The pain continued for the next several months, and there was little to no improvement with the treatments he had received. His primary doctor decided to order a CT scan of his chest, given his lifelong history of smoking. The results showed the cause of his pain: a tumor in his upper right lung that spread into the lymph nodes in the mid chest region. Bill always had a fatalistic approach to life and decided he would accept chemotherapy and radiation treatments but wasn't about to give up his cigarettes. We had journeyed down to see him in January of my final year and attempted to get him into some therapy trials through UC San Diego. I had interviewed there for both emergency medicine and pulmonary—critical care medicine and had met the chair of pulmonary medicine. I called him up and described Bill's situation. He immediately agreed to evaluate him and enroll him in any trials for which he might be eligible. As we left to return home to Davis, I made Bill promise he would make it to my medical school graduation six months later. He told me he would do whatever it took to be there.

Despite facing his probable life—ending cancer, he continued to smoke two packs per day, even with supplemental oxygen in the house. He did, however, keep his promise to me and came to my graduation with the assistance of Susan's aunt and uncle as well as her mother, Doris. When I saw him, he looked so emaciated and short of breath and was barely walking on his own. His trademark cigarette, however, was hanging from his fingers out on the front porch of our house.

By August of 1992, he was wasting away and it was clear he was losing the battle. I had started my second rotation of internship in internal medicine, and Susan was in daily contact with her mom about Bill's status. In mid August, he got to the point of needing admission to the hospital, so Susan flew down that weekend to support her mother as well as to spend the last days with her father. On a Monday morning, the nurse caring for Bill called their house and told Doris, Susan's mother, that he was fading quickly and acting as though he wanted to die. Susan drove them both to the hospital and entered the room. Bill was too weak to talk much, but Susan held his hand and told him it was okay to go. Suddenly, Bill tried to sit up and get out of bed, as though he was going to walk across to the other side.

Susan calmed him and told him, "No, Daddy. Just lay back and let go."

Bill relaxed and, within a minute or two, slipped away as Susan held his hand.

My pager went off in the middle of morning rounds, and I knew it wasn't going to be good news. I excused myself from the group and called Susan at her parent's house. She told me that her father had just died a few minutes ago while she and her mother were at his side. It had been such a peaceful and gentle death, and she was so grateful to God that she was able to be there and send him off. I told her I would leave the hospital and pick the kids up at our house to begin the drive down to San Diego.

I had been keeping the attending physician on my rotation as well as the senior resident informed of Bill's eminent death, so there was no problem leaving at a moment's notice. I signed my patients out to the resident and drove quickly home to load up the kids and our suitcases. By this time, David was fifteen and Christy was twelve, so I felt comfortable leaving them at home during the summer vacation with Susan away in San Diego. I sat them both down and explained that Grandpa Bill had died peacefully with Grandma Doris and Susan at his side.

When we arrived at her parent's home, Susan's sister and brother—in—law had already arrived from the Imperial Valley. Susan explained how they had made all the arrangements for a graveside funeral in two days, knowing I had to return as soon as I could to my hospital duties. I asked if there was going to be any kind of religious service or eulogy. The funeral home had arranged for the pastor of a local church to officiate, but I knew that the only things he would know about Bill were whatever Doris and the family could tell him. I asked Doris if she would mind me giving a short eulogy as I knew Bill personally since I had met Susan in 1971. She was surprised and gratified that I would do that for him, so I spent the next two days reflecting on what this man had meant in my life. He had always been rather aloof and introverted his whole life, and the only time he became outgoing was with alcohol in his system. His whole life had been spent in the military as a youth and in the civil service as an inspector of navy helicopters. He worked at North Island Naval Air Station in the middle of San Diego Harbor and would inspect helicopters that had been repaired or serviced. I vividly remember Bill and Doris answering the door when I showed up at their house to take Susan on our first date during the summer before our senior year in high school. I was somewhat intimidated and felt as though I was being inspected like one of his helicopters. In reality, I was Susan's first real boyfriend and they were eager to meet me.

I spoke at the funeral about all of these memories and then mentioned that Bill had given me the greatest gift of my life. On April 19, 1975, he gave me his baby daughter's hand in marriage. He had been a great father—in—law through the years and had taught Susan and me to play Pinochle, a WWII favorite card game. Bill was an ace at the game; and the few times I was able to out game him, I would glow with pride. I ended the eulogy by talking about how we all have vices in life and that Bill's one major vice, besides smoking and drinking, was betting on horse races. I noted that he was probably in heaven right now, placing wagers on races. The only difference, however, was that now he knew which horse was going to win before the race had even started.

In early 2003, Susan and I took our mothers on a trip to Reno, Nevada, for a mid—winter getaway and some gambling at the casinos. For several weeks prior to the trip, my mom had been coughing persistently and uncontrollably at times. She was also feeling short of breath when exerting herself. I told her she needed to see her doctor and make sure she didn't have pneumonia. One of the days on the trip, we drove to Virginia City, an old silver—mining town that still has the appearance of a Wild West settlement. There are wooden sidewalks, old houses, and an old boot hill type cemetery. Neither of our mothers had been in the past, so we knew they would enjoy the diversion from the slot machines. While driving on one of the old streets for some last minute sightseeing before we drove back to Reno, my mother began coughing intractably in the backseat and then exclaimed, "Oh my God!"

I slowed to the side of the street and turned around to see her holding a blood—soaked wad of tissues. "Is this the first time you've coughed up blood?" I asked her.

She replied to my inquiry that it was the first time, and I quickly told her she needed to get into see her doctor as soon as we returned to the Sacramento area in two days. I talked about all the things that needed to be checked out, making sure she didn't have tuberculosis, pneumonia, or bleeding problems. I avoided naming the one diagnosis that I most suspected she had: some type of lung cancer. We stayed one more night, but I had a difficult time enjoying myself with what had occurred earlier in the day.

That next week, my mom was set up by her primary doctor for a CT scan of the chest, which showed a large area of right lower lung pneumonia but no clear mass. She then was referred to see a pulmonologist. The pulmonologist was someone I had trained with at UC Davis Medical Center and knew quite well. She was scheduled for a bronchoscopy after her visit with the doctor, which is a procedure to guide a camera into the airways and identify the cause of the bleeding and coughing.

The morning of the procedure, I took off work and accompanied my parents to the hospital. I knew, after seeing a copy of her CT scan, that she had a large tumor mass in her right lower lobe of her lungs. The pulmonologist performed the bronchoscopy, along with taking biopsies from the mass and additional lesions lining her trachea. She had stage IV squamous cell lung cancer. It had spread along her airways, into her lymph nodes, and possibly into distant parts of her body. I began to pray that God would allow her more time but steeled myself for the likely decline to death over the next couple of months.

My mother is my hero. She taught me that what medical science cannot do, God certainly can when you rely on Him through prayer. She started combination therapy of daily radiation treatments to the lungs and mediastinum (the middle part of the chest where the trachea, heart, esophagus, and lymph nodes are located). This was combined with only one chemo agent, Taxol, a milder drug with fewer side effects. I knew that without a multi—drug regimen, her chances of survival were very low, but I believed the oncologist wanted to spare her from the ravaging of stronger chemo drugs, given the likelihood she would die from this lung cancer over the next few months.

She got through the thirty—five radiation treatments with the usual side effects of skin burns and irritation to the esophagus, making eating and drinking painfully difficult. Every day, she woke up and thanked God for another day of life and just took things as they came. Slowly but surely, she finished her chemo, started recovering, and had a post—treatment chest CT scan to restage her tumor. Miraculously, the tumor was in remission and no new masses were found. Months went by; and then, before long, we were counting years and every study came back negative. My mother is now over five years out from her diagnosis and remains cancer free. This constitutes a cure and, in the words of her oncologist, a miracle. My hero had shown me what faith and prayer could accomplish, even if I didn't believe she would beat it.

PUTTING MY FAITH
TO WORK

It has often been said that God never gives us more adversity than we can handle, even though sometimes it feels like He's piling it on. When I went through my bout with head and neck cancer as a second—year medical student, it was very clear to me that God had a purpose with that diagnosis and treatment path I had to follow. It was my wake—up call about prioritizing my wife and family above everything except my faith and the lesson that all of the success and glory I accomplished in medical school was His doing, not mine. One of the losses I went through with that first bout of cancer was my clear speech and strong voice. I had grown up playing the guitar and singing and enjoyed play-ing and singing in the folk group at our parish in San Diego. I had given that up when we moved to Davis for medical school and believed it was something I couldn't make time for, as I was always focusing on my classes and studying. I found out the hard way that it is true you don't know what you have until it is taken away from you.

In 2002, I noticed a mole on my right foot that I didn't remember being there in the past. I even thought to myself, "Could this be a malignant melanoma?" I kept a close eye on it over a few weeks, and when it started looking red around the border, I decided it was time to have my dermatologist take a look at it.

I dropped by his office one day at lunchtime and asked him to take a look at the lesion.

As soon as he saw it, he said, "I think we'll do a punch biopsy on this little devil."

I asked him if he thought it could be melanoma, and he replied that it did look suspicious but we would see the results of the biopsy. A couple of days later, while wrapping up an evening shift in the ER, I decided to check to see if the biopsy result was back. I pulled it up on the computer, and read, "Final Diagnosis: Melanoma in Situ." Panic ran through my brain, knowing that melanomas typically spread rapidly and aggressively. I was slightly relieved to see the "in situ" part, which meant that there was no evidence of spread beyond the skin surface. I was amazed at that since I had been watching the lesion for close to two months prior to going in to see the dermatologist. When I got home late that night after finishing the shift, I woke Susan up and told her the news. We hugged each other, cried together, and then decided that we would leave it in God's hands. After all, we had been through cancer together before and we could get through it again.

The next day, Tom, the dermatologist, called me to report out the results to me. I told him I had already seen it and asked where we went from there. The standard approach for in—situ lesions, especially on the extremities, is wide excision and monitoring without lymph node dissection farther up the leg.

Our chief of podiatry, a nationally known surgeon who is well—published in the field, performed the surgery. The melanoma was located on the top of my foot, between the bases of the third and fourth toes. It required a rotational flap to cover the skin deficit, and I awoke from surgery to find my right leg in a short leg cast to keep the foot still. Any excess movement would possibly stretch or tear the flap. This would be a disaster since the flap would likely die, causing a bigger area to need a skin graft. I toughed out three weeks of immobilization and not being able to work. When the cast was removed, it took a few days to recover my flexibility and muscle tone, but I got back to work without any problems. The only sign of the melanoma and treatment is a faint, crescent—shaped scar across the distal end of my right foot. I also now make sure I wear a factor 30 or more sunscreen when out in the sun for any length of time.

THE BIGGEST CHALLENGE
OF MY LIFE

In November of 2005, we were blessed to attend the wedding of my son David's best friend from high school, Fernando. He was a Venezuelan citizen and had come to live with his aunt, a naturalized immigrant, in Davis to attend high school in the US. Fernando returned to Caracas when he finished high school, and David went with him to meet his family and spend a couple of months in the country. They had made a promise they would be each other's best men when they got to the point of marrying someone.

Several years later, Fernando called David and told him he was engaged to his girlfriend whom he had been dating for the prior several months. Fernando scheduled his wedding to a beautiful Latin lady, Annie, over the Thanksgiving holiday. Fernando also wanted Susan and me to attend since we had been his surrogate parents during high school. Three days before Thanksgiving, me, Susan, David, and his girlfriend, Michelle, all took off for Venezuela.

The trip was a crazy schedule of more airplane flights than we had ever tried to cram into a seven—day period in our entire lives. We flew across the US on two separate Southwest Airlines flights since we had some free flights from using our Southwest credit card. The airline doesn't fly into Miami, so we flew to Fort Lauderdale and rented a one—way car to drive down to the Miami International Airport. We flew almost four hours on Thanksgiving Day from Miami to Caracas on Aeropostale, the national carrier for Venezuela. Fernando was picking us up for the drive into the city from the coastal location of the airport. He was driving his future mother—in—law's SUV since he didn't own a car of his own. The traffic on the freeway over the mountain and into the valley Caracas sits in was the worst I had ever seen in my entire life. Each side of the highway was five or six lanes, but the concept of separate lanes didn't apply to any of the drivers. Cars would merge into a two—foot space if they could wedge their bumper into the space before you forced them out. The flow of cars was so slow that there were vendors walking in all the lanes and open spaces, hawking newspapers, cold drinks, snacks, and anything else a trapped driver might want or need. The climax of our first ride in a car in Venezuela was the point when Fernando rear—ended the car in front of him. It was three teen-age boys driving their mother's car. When Fernando got out to talk with them, he told us to remain in the car and he would handle it. Fernando checked the bumpers and saw it was just a few minor scratches on both cars. No police were ever called, and Fernando talked the teens into accepting his contact information written on a slip of paper. He quickly changed lanes and drove away, explaining that he had given them false identifying information and didn't want to allow them enough time to write down the license number of his mother—in—law's car. Such is the way accidents are handled in Venezuela.

Annie's parents were very well off, living in a nice section of the suburbs. Her stepfather was a gastroenterologist at the university hospital; and her mother, Carolina, worked for the social services division of the federal government. Carolina had her live—in maid prepare an authentic American Thanksgiving dinner for us, including roast turkey, mashed potatoes, peas, cranberry sauce, and homemade stuffing. The meal was topped off by tres leches cake, a dessert to die for that we had never had before. David was the only one who had tasted it before, during his summer trip after high school.

The wedding was being held at an all—inclusive resort named Coche Paradise. It was a small island off the east coast of Venezuela, just south of Isla Margarita, a well—known resort destination. We caught another flight out of Caracas to Margarita and then a forty—five—minute boat ride to Coche Paradise.

The wedding was a beautiful evening Catholic mass in the resort's chapel, with an all—night reception on the beach. The festivities included unlimited dancing, with the dinner served around 10:00 p.m. and the cake finally cut sometime after midnight. The next day was our return flight to Caracas, with our flight to Miami the following day. We essentially reproduced our route to the wedding when we returned home. It ended up being seven different flights in nine days, with two boat rides thrown in just to round out the trip.

About two weeks after the trip, I developed a hacking, persistent cough that sounded suspiciously like the cough of a rather overweight man who had been sitting behind me on the flight from Fort Lauderdale to Sacramento. He coughed incessantly the whole trip, spewing a fog of respiratory secretions over the seat, my head, and into my lap. I didn't have a fever and never produced any sputum, so I ignored it, assuming it was a viral upper respiratory infection that would resolve on its own.

The cough continued to nag me into December and January, but that wasn't unusual for the winter months in Davis. I got up the morning of Valentine's Day, February 14, 2006, and jumped into the shower to get ready for some meetings and administrative work later that morning. I had become the chief of our ER at the beginning of 2003 and had a lot of non—clinical duties that I oversaw in my role. I started my usual morning episode of coughing when I coughed up a moderate amount of blood into the shower floor. I knew this couldn't be good and was either tuberculosis or cancer. I told Susan about it before leaving for the hospital, as I didn't want to hit her with a bad diagnosis without any warning.

I went in and found my assistant chief, Rodney, working a shift. I told him what had occurred and asked if he would see me as a patient. He agreed and ordered a chest x—ray to initially evaluate me. The x—ray didn't show a distinct mass but did show some suspicious irregularity behind my heart border and along the mediastinum where all the lymph nodes were located. The chief of radiology reviewed it with me and said the next step would be a CT scan of my chest to evaluate what was causing the shadowing.

The CT scan was clearly diagnostic of the cause of my coughing up blood earlier in the morning. I had a golf—ball—sized mass in my left lower lung lobe and enlarged lymph nodes along the left main stem bronchus. I called Susan and told her I most likely had lung cancer eerily similar to my mother's. It broke my heart to ruin our Valentine's Day with such ominous news, but she had to know about it as soon as possible. One of my colleagues, who trained me during residency and was a pulmonologist, scheduled me for a bronchoscopy in the early afternoon. I would be sedated for the procedure, so I needed Susan to come to the hospital to drive me home after the exam was completed.

Biopsies taken from some of the lymph nodes indicated probable squamouscell carcinoma. This was the same type of cancer my mother had endured and survived and also the same as my original head and neck cancer. There was no relation between my two cancers since they were almost two decades apart, but I obviously had a predisposition for this type of cancer. My cancer wasn't as advanced as hers, as I was staged at IIIA. It still was inoperable, however, and would require chemotherapy and radiation therapy to give me any chance to survive it.

Being a physician has its pluses and minuses in a situation like mine. I was able to expedite a workup in less than eight hours that took my mother or any other non—medically connected patient two or more weeks to get done. The down side, however, is that I had access to data and studies that most patients never see. I was very aware that the chance of my surviving this lung cancer was less than 10 to 15 percent, taking into account the stage, my age, and the length of time I had the tumor without being aware of it or receiving treatment.

What these statistics didn't take into account however, was the spiritual relationship I had with God and the role that prayer would play in the battle.

That same night, Susan and I were due to attend the weekly meeting of the RCIA program at church. The class culminates on the Easter vigil, the night prior to Easter Sunday, when the candidates receive their sacraments and are welcomed into the full body of the Catholic church.

Those who were never baptized as a Christian are baptized during the mass. Along with the candidates who have been baptized at a prior time, such as a baby, or with a different Christian church, all members of the RCIA are confirmed as neophytes, or new members of the church. They also receive their first Holy Communion. It's a long mass, lasting almost three hours, but is one of the most beautiful nights in the church.

In September of 2005, we had agreed to sponsor two older adults who wanted to fully join the church. I say older since a majority of the attendees are college age and attending UC Davis. My candidate, Frank, was about my age and needed to join the rest of his family in the Catholic faith. His wife was already a member of the church, and both of his daughters had been raised in the faith their whole lives. Frank had been baptized in another Protestant faith but wanted to share the Catholic faith with the rest of his family.

I agonized about whether to attend that night and how or if to share the diagnosis with the group. I prayed about it all afternoon and finally decided that the sooner they knew the sooner they could start praying for me. The irony was that my daughter and future son—in—law were attending that year's class too.

Christy had met Steve about four years earlier and fallen in love with him. It was an easy answer for her when he proposed to her in the summer of 2005. The only hitch was that Steve had never been baptized and had no spiritual faith growing up. Christy very much wanted to get married in the Catholic Church, so Steve told her he would do whatever he had to in order for that to happen. He didn't have to be a Catholic to marry her in the church, but he did have to be baptized.

They wanted a destination wedding in Lake Tahoe, so we took a trip together in July to check out churches in the area. There were two or three on the California side of the lake, but none met their expectations for beauty and adequate size for a large group. The very last church we looked at was located at Incline Village on the Nevada side. We pulled up to Saint Francis of Assisi Catholic Church on Saturday afternoon and checked the door on the side, next to the parking lot. As we entered the church, we were all stunned and immediately knew this was it. The back of the altar was all large, plate—glass windows with an unbelievable view of the pine trees, Lake Tahoe, and the western Sierras behind the lake. There was still a little snow capping the mountains that July. The church itself was wood framed with a warm feeling of home to all of us.

I had noticed as we came in the side door that there was a staircase leading down to a lower level and a sign indicating that it was the location of the parish office. Taking a chance that somebody might be there on a late Saturday afternoon, I went down and noticed a man with his back turned to me in a windowed office, feverishly typing on a computer. I knocked on the door jam and startled him briefly. He turned around and asked how he could help me. I introduced myself and told him we weren't members of the parish but were looking for a location for our daughter's wedding in a year and had immediately fallen in love with the church. He graciously told me that he was Father Bill and was the new pastor of the parish. He had been in the position for all of three weeks. Father Bill was actually called out of retirement to shepherd the parish. The majority of his thirty—five years of priesthood had been as a Catholic chaplain to several prisons in Nevada. I excused myself for one minute and ran up to get Susan, Christy, and Steve.

We sat and talked with Father Bill about having the wedding at his new parish. One major question was the Catholic policy that you should be married in your home parish. Father Bill didn't think it was an issue in his mind and actually felt that anything that encouraged young people to be married in the Catholic Church should be acceptable without debate. We had him put the date on his calendar and that of the church so we could know it would be reserved for next summer.

Driving home, Steve announced to us that he wanted to go through the RCIA process and be a confirmed Catholic by the time of the wedding. Not wanting him to feel pressured, we assured him that he didn't have to go that far. He just needed to get himself baptized wherever he felt the most comfortable. He replied that after seeing Saint Francis Parish, he wanted to be fully Catholic when he and Christy were married there. So, Steve and Christy, as his sponsor, started RCIA in September 2005 and would finish on the Easter Vigil in April 2006.

After deciding to tell the RCIA group about my Valentine's Day diagnosis, I knew I didn't want Steve and Christy finding out in that setting. I called both David and Christy that afternoon and broke the news to them. Steve was just walking in the door from work when he was met by an anguished scream from Christy as she listened to me tell her the situation. Christy was crying profusely; but I assured her that no matter what happened, I would be at her wedding one way or another. I also called my candidate I was sponsoring, Frank, before he left his house to let him know about my diagnosis and my plan to share it at that evening's class.

Christy and Steve came to our house before the class started, and we talked about the plan to tell the class. The four of us drove to the church and arrived a few minutes early. I pulled a couple of the RCIA team leaders aside and broke the news to them. They were stunned but agreed to give me time before the class began to break the news to the whole group. Steve and Suzanne, two of the main leaders, opened the class by saying Susan and I needed a few minutes to share some news with them. We got up in front of the group, some of whom we barely knew and others we had gotten to know deeply in spiritual discussions and group sharing.

I said a brief, silent prayer asking the Holy Spirit to guide my words and help me tell the group without sounding like I was asking for pity. I began the conversation, saying, "God has worked in our lives over and over again throughout the years, both in good times and bad. Today, I found out he was asking me to rely on my faith and trust in him one more time. This morning, I was diagnosed with lung cancer."

A loud gasp erupted from one woman in the group and Steve, Christy, and Susan, standing next to me, all began to cry. I held my own tears back and told the group that I needed their prayers and support over the coming weeks and months. I promised them I would be at the

Easter vigil to help celebrate their rites of baptism, confirmation, and full participation in the Catholic mass. I had spoken with our pastor, Father Dan, earlier in the evening and asked him to perform an anointing of the sick for me the following Wednesday, before the start of the RCIA class. He agreed to do it, so I invited any members of the team, sponsors, or candidates to come early if they felt comfortable attending. I was humbled to see over 90 percent of the group arrive an hour before the start of the class to be present for this Sacrament from Father Dan. As mentioned previously, anointing of the sick used to be known as last rites and was given to those very near death or who had just passed. With the changes in the Church doctrine after Vatican II, it now was given to any ill or suffering Catholic who requested the Sacrament.

Father Dan said a few opening prayers and then asked me to unbutton my shirt. He anointed my bare chest with the oil of chrism and pushed, actually quite hard, on my sternum. Asking God to heal me, he also invited those in the group to lay hands on me and pray for the same. I was touched deeply by all the love and concern showered upon me that evening and felt calm as I began my chemotherapy toward the end of that week.

My oncologists put me on an aggressive regimen consisting of a dose of Cisplatin every two to three weeks, with Etoposide weekly and daily radiation to my chest on Monday through Friday for a total of thirty—five treatments. Initially, I didn't feel too many effects from the regimen and was even elated to find that, after three weeks of treatment, I still had my hair. That elation was short lived, however, when, during the fourth week, I found my hair falling out in large chunks during a morning shower. I showed Susan my new checkerboard patchwork of bare scalp, and we decided I should clipper the rest off. Christy came over and helped me do the deed; and actually, my head didn't look too bad with the bald coiffure. I began wearing a baseball cap to protect my scalp from bumps, bangs, and sunburn.

Radiation is an interesting phenomenon to ask the human body to endure. Early in the course, as with my head and neck cancer in the late 1980s, I felt nothing from the treatment and only had some slight redness to the skin. By the end of the thirty—five treatments, however, it was a different story. I was having extreme difficulty swallowing, with burning pain in my esophagus as I tried to eat. Radiation esophagitis is one of the common side effects from radiation therapy to any body location where the esophagus lies in the field of treatment. This was true for my neck radiation in 1989 and also true for my lung radiation during this course. This time around, however, it seemed worse than I remembered. I tried numerous homeopathic remedies but was having so much pain eating that I was starting to lose weight. I was able to somewhat tolerate Ensure supplements, but even those caused excruciating pain. We tried numbing the esophagus before meals with Mylanta and viscous Lidocaine, but this gave very little relief to the pain. I finally decided I would let go and let God just get me through this trial to bear. People and friends would ask me how I was doing; and my reply was, "They haven't nailed me to a cross yet."

One day, after one of the last radiation episodes, we decided to go to lunch at a restaurant and I would eat as much as I could tolerate. To drink with my lunch, I ordered an iced tea. Sipping it slowly, I found that the tea didn't cause any pain or irritation. When my soft sandwich arrived, I experimented with drinking a gulp of tea and then taking a bite of food. Amazingly, I had very little pain, if any, as I swallowed the bite. It was such a simple solution that had been before me all the time and just took the right circumstance to see it.

Slowly but surely, my body was able to heal and I began to regain the weight I had lost. My burned, radiated chest healed with time and got back to the point where the only evidence of my cancer were tiny, pinpoint tattoos that were placed for alignment marks to use with the laser on the linear accelerator that generates the radiation beam. My hair grew back thicker than ever and even with less gray in it than I had prior to chemotherapy.

It took the rest of 2006 to fully recover to the point of returning to work. Every day, I would wake up and praise God for another day of life and the blessings of being able to spend time with my family. I also was truly grateful for being able to continue on in my vocation as a physician. I still, to this day, thank God, every day, through prayer, for each and every blessing of life he gives us.

THE YEAR OF WEDDINGS

Two thousand and six, besides seeing me recover from the treatments for lung cancer, became the year of weddings for our family. Christy and Steve had been planning, for over one year, their matrimony at Saint Francis of Assisi Church in Lake Tahoe on July 22, 2006. The wedding became a massive production with over two hundred guests in attendance. We rented two large cabins, which were actually houses, on the Nevada side of the lake. One house was for our extended family to use, and the other was reserved for the wedding party. The weather was extremely warm that July, but we all enjoyed the time together. We set up a golf game the Friday before the wedding date, and Steve's dad and family joined me and Chuck along with a couple of my friends who played too.

When we had looked into wedding cakes for two hundred people, I was astounded to find that it would cost anywhere from $900 to $1200 from a bakery. We went to the region's biggest market that had a bakery. They could make a very nice three—tier cake to feed two hundred people for $350. The downside was that it had to be picked up on the morning of the wedding and transported to the golf course lodge we had rented for the reception. The plan was for David and I to take my car and get the cake transported to the reception site. We would do this before we got dressed in our tuxedos to go to the church. We loaded the cake in the back of my SUV, carefully transferring the box to the rear cargo area of the car. The bakery manager reinforced that because it was tiered, I should drive very slowly, especially around corners, as they couldn't be responsible if any tiers slipped in transit. I drove as slow as I could, and all stops were made very carefully and methodically. There was one left turn where the road sloped away from the turn and led up to the clubhouse/lodge.

David and I pulled into a covered overhang, and I asked him to go inside and look for a cart we could load it onto for transport. I opened the back door and lifted the lid on the cake box just before David went inside the lodge.

"Oh my God!" I shouted, as I called David to come look at the cake.

"Quit screwing around, Dad. We don't have much time to get back and get ready for the wedding," David replied.

"No," I told him. "Come and look, as we've got a really big problem."

The top two tiers had slid about two inches to the side of the base, exposing cake, broken frosting, and my horror as I thought about Christy's anguish when she saw what happened. We left the cake there and ran in to find the wedding coordinator. Bringing her out with a cart, she thought the head cook might be able to fix it. We showed him the mess of the cake, and he wasn't very optimistic. He left to try to find several large spatulas, and I told David I was going to try something. I tipped the box carefully toward the side the cake had slid from and gently began shaking. The cake started to move back into place. Just then, the kitchen manager returned, unable to find enough spatulas to lift the top tiers. I showed him what I had been able to do, and to my shock, he grabbed the edge of the box and gave the cake one big shake and, amazingly, the cake landed back in perfect position. I had envisioned him shaking the top tiers apart with the force he used. Now, the only issue was to hide the break in the frosting, so he mixed up some white whipped cream and did the repair.

The wedding was everything Christy and Steve had hoped for, and everybody was impressed with Father Bill as he officiated. He had Steve and Christy come up around the altar and receive communion as a couple before the rest of the guests. The wedding party left the church in a limousine to do a trip around Incline Village and the lake for wedding photos. The rest of us headed to the clubhouse for the reception. When

I looked at the cake, I could tell some repair work had been done, but it really came out okay when I thought of what that cake looked like in the back of car. Christy never noticed it, and I didn't tell her until after the cake had been cut and served.

The hardest part for me was delivering the father of the bride speech and keeping from crying. I did a little at first but pulled myself together enough to get through it. I related to everyone how, when Christy was a sick infant and going through her first shunts, followed by the open heart surgery at four, the vision of her in a white gown at her wedding was the image Susan and I focused on to help us get through it. I talked about how we first met Steve when Christy was in the hospital after an appendectomy. They were supposed to have had their first date the night before, but Christy was being admitted for surgery. Steve drove all the way from Chico, where he attended college, and sat by her side all day long the day after her operation. He won our hearts that first meeting by the tenderness and care he showed our daughter, helping her up to the restroom, getting her water, and just generally being there for her. By the time I finished my speech, there was not a dry eye in the room, mine included.

David had a long series of girlfriends before he met his wife, Michelle. Being in a band and playing at nightclubs around Sacramento exposed him to a lot of band groupies, and he seemed to always attract the pretty blondes with emotional or personality issues. One was actually a lesbian and hadn't revealed this to David until after he had moved in with her. She had used him as leverage with her parents, who lived in Wisconsin, to convince her father to buy her a house in Sacramento. Another was very nice but was going through an extremely difficult time with a younger brother who was dying of a rare cancer that had invaded the nervous system. She requested my assistance with family conferences and meetings with the doctors to help her father accept the prognosis. Susan and I ended up attending the funeral for the unfortunate young man.

We told David that he had to be with a girl for at least one year before we wanted to meet her parents. There had been too much emotional turmoil with his trials and tribulations. Michelle came along just in time to help David get out of a depression tailspin. She had come to one of his shows with a close girlfriend who was supposed to be meeting David after they had corresponded on a social media website. David ended up being attracted to Michelle, however, and they talked all night after the show. She was not a flashy blonde or carrying a lot of baggage. Michelle was a nice young woman with natural, dark red hair. She was also the smartest girlfriend he ever had and even got us a little miffed when she started coming to our family game nights. Michelle knew the answers to every Trivial Pursuit and movie game question. She would win all the time, unabashedly. We came to really like her, however, especially when she traveled with us to Hawaii for a family vacation. It took a lot of bravery to stay for ten days with a family she barely knew, that included my parents and Susan's mother.

David and Michelle lived together for several years before they set their wedding date. They too wanted a 2006 wedding in the fall of that year. I found out that he and Christy had planned it this way so I wouldn't miss their weddings if my cancer battle was lost.

They set their wedding date for October 14, 2006 and, as opposed to the massive event for Steve and Christy's, they just wanted a small gathering of close relatives, friends, and co—workers. The wedding was held in a vineyard up in the foothills near Auburn. I still laugh when I look at the video of the ceremony and can distinctly hear a cow mooing behind their vows. The reception was at a very nice restaurant in Roseville in a crowded but intimate banquet room. I really enjoyed the chance I had to make a reception video for them, starting with the wedding photos of Michelle's parents and Susan and I. It continued with photos of them as toddlers, children, and teenagers, culminating in photos taken right before the wedding. All of this was set to contemporary songs for the periods of the photographs. We sent them off in an antique limousine, and they honeymooned in the Cabo San Lucas region, just relaxing and being together as a newly married couple.

RETURN TO PHYSICIANHOOD

In the autumn of 2006, before returning to work in 2007, we decided, on the spur of the moment, to take a trip to the Canadian Rockies. The farthest north we had ever been was Vancouver in prior trips to Canada. One of our younger ER physicians, Trevor, is a Canadian, and he gave me the whole scoop on what to see and visit. We drove north, stopping for a couple of days to hang around Vancouver, and then pressed on in a northeast direction to see Whistler. There was no snow yet but lots of BMX downhill bikers riding the dirt ski slopes. Our trip took us across and up to the ice fields and our northernmost destination of Jasper, Alberta. We came upon a cute set of cabins just south of Jasper. Since we had no timeline on this trip, we stopped and rented one of the cabins for two nights. The cabins were built in a circle around a large grass area with a playground. Walking across the grass the afternoon we checked in, we noticed a lot of scattered droppings all over. I commented to Susan that there must be some animal or animals that frequent the grass park, but couldn't tell from the droppings if they were deer or some other large animals.

That evening, we walked to the restaurant run by the owners of the resort and had an exquisite sunset dinner. After sharing a bottle of wine, we decided to return to our cabin and start the fire that had been cozily prepared in the fireplace of our unit. As we walked around the perimeter of the cabins, I was startled to see a large female elk sauntering between parked cars. I told Susan that must explain the animal droppings in the grass park. We turned between our cabin and the next one over and were completed stunned to see a herd of about thirty to forty elk, including bulls and calves, lying on and grazing on the grass field. One female was firmly planted about fifteen feet from our front door, the only entrance to the cabin. We quietly stepped in between her and the door and acted cool and confident as we unlocked the door and slipped inside.

"Wow!" I shouted to Susan. Other than trips to Yellowstone National Park, we had never seen that many elk gathered in one spot.

When we arose to go to breakfast in the morning, I looked out the window of the cabin, and the entire herd had moved on sometime before dawn. The other night we stayed at this beautiful resort, they returned, after sunset, to sleep in their protected sanctuary. After a great breakfast at the restaurant, we decided to drive back north and into Jasper to check out the shops and small train museum. After turning north, back onto Icefields Parkway, I saw what appeared to be a large dog slowly crossing the road. As we approached, I realized it was a beautiful silver wolf who ambled across the highway and along the side of the road for several hundred yards. We were able to get fantastic candid photos of this most stunning of God's creatures before he headed up a hill into the thick forest.

Jasper is a quaint Canadian town with lots of rustic shops and restaurants and represents the far north end of Icefields Parkway on Alberta Highway 93. We had a nice lunch in Jasper and drove around the area before returning to our cabin and our elk companions for the night. The next day, we packed up and began our slow, leisurely tour of Icefields Parkway, marveling at incredible glaciers, sky—high mountain peaks still covered in snow after the spring and summer melt, and keeping our eyes peeled for more animals. The Columbia Icefields, and in particular, Athabasca Glacier, was astounding. We stopped and hiked to the lower edge of the glacier and walked out as far as we could, limited by a rope perimeter that had been staked out by the national park rangers. Susan was ahead of me and jauntily strode out onto the ice with a quick pace. When I got to the edge, I stepped up and onto the glacier and immediately felt like I could slip, fall, and hit my head on the ice flow. I had worn some shoes with a rubber sole but no deep tread, and every step or movement of my feet felt extremely slippery. I got all of about twenty feet onto the ice and called Susan back to help stabilize me as I walked back toward the wooden pathway. We continued south on the parkway after taking several dozen photos of the glacier. Every turn was a new photo stop, with mountains, waterfalls, and small glaciers to be seen and recorded. We finally got to the small road up to Lake Louise and watched the late—afternoon sun bounce off the glacier behind the lake and the pristine, icy waters of Lake Louise. We took a short walk on a trail along the north side of the lake but cowardly turned back after reading a sign that the wilderness area around Lake Louise contains the largest concentration of grizzly bears in the world. Commenting to another tourist on the trail about this disturbing sign, she related how the day before, a grizzly had wandered through the cafeteria at the lake visitor center and helped itself to food, drink, and anything else it desired. We decided to get back on the road and search out a great hotel to stay at in Banff.

After leaving Canada, we traveled through Montana and had wanted to stay in Glacier National Park. On arrival to the ranger station, we found the road had been closed by a rockslide and we wouldn't be able to drive through the park. Rather than drive up into the mountains just to turn around, we pressed on to Bozeman and stayed in a rustic hotel. The next day, we drove into the Little Bighorn Battlefield Monument and spent several hours learning about how General Custer's planned massacre of the Oglala and other Sioux nations turned into a slaughter of his entire battalion, along with him, when he grossly underestimated the collection of Sioux warriors encamped in the crook of the Little Bighorn River valley. It is a sobering drive through the battlefield and made us wonder what it will take for the world to learn to love one another; share the resources of our lands; and seek God rather than power, glory, and domination of others.

After Montana and Wyoming, we continued onto the Black Hills of South Dakota to visit Mount Rushmore. We spent one night in Deadwood and drove the next morning to the monument. Rounding a corner in the trees, the first view we had of Rushmore was somewhat disappointing. The figures on the mountain seemed a lot smaller than we were expecting, but we soon found it was an optical illusion. Driving up to the parking lot at the base of Mount Rushmore, you are stunned at the enormity of the four presidents immortalized on the mountain and the enormous pile of blasted, jack—hammered, and chiseled granite at the bottom. The day we were there, a ranger team of maintenance workers were on the heads, rappelling onto the facial features and doing very dangerous restoration and preservation work on the rock faces.

Equally, or even more impressive, was the Crazy Horse memorial. This is a partially completed monument to honor Crazy Horse, an Oglala—Lakota Sioux warrior. Located seventeen miles from Mount Rushmore, the project was started in 1948 by a Polish American sculptor named Korczak Ziolkowski. He had been one of the sculptors who worked on Mount Rushmore and was contacted in 1939 by Chief Henry Standing Bear of the Sioux nation. In a letter to Ziolkowski, the chief stated in part, "My fellow chiefs and I would like the white man to know that the red man has great heroes too." The monument has been partially sculpted to date, with the head, face, and parts of the pointing arm of Crazy Horse visible. It is over four times the size of Mount Rushmore and has been sculpted by only Ziolkowski, his children, and a few hired hands. No financial support from the US government has been used, and the family actually turned down a $10,000,000 grant offered by the federal government. The vast majority of financial support comes from donations from other Native American nations as well as the park fees paid by visitors.

The return from our trip took us across Wyoming, Utah, and Nevada back to California. It was such a gift for Susan and me to be free of cares about chemotherapy, radiation, and recovering from cancer and to just travel together and take in the beauty of our western United States. It's amazing that when you leave California, the west is very unpopulated, vast, and natural except for a few medium—sized cities. During our trip home, we kept noticing numerous deerlike animals hopping across the open plains. They were much smaller than deer, and then it finally dawned on us. These were North American pronghorn antelope made famous in the old cowboy song that starts out with, "Oh give me a home, where the buffalo roam, and the deer and the antelope play." We were constantly amazed by the diversity of God's creation and the number of native animals still running free in our populated country.

By the end of 2006, I felt close to being back to normal after the numerous chemotherapy doses and associated radiation therapy in the spring. I decided I would return to work fulltime starting on January 1, 2007. It was difficult at first, as I had lost a lot of stamina and had some chronic pulmonary problems due to the scarring and radiation changes in my lungs. Overall, however, I was so thankful to be alive and have no evidence of active cancer in follow—up studies. It felt so good to be a doctor again and be able to care for patients instead of being the patient myself.

I resigned my position as the chief of the emergency department; and the assistant chief and my good friend, Rodney, took the position after having been the interim chief during my absence. Rodney is one of the calmest, most balanced individuals I have ever met, and I knew he could manage the department well. Right before my diagnosis in February of 2006, I had become, in addition to the department chief, the assistant physician in chief of the medical center over emergency and trauma services. With my return to work after treatment, I knew it would be too much to try to perform both leadership roles, so I told my supervisor, Rich, the physician in chief, that I would continue on as his assistant in the APIC role but needed to step down as the department chief. Rich was agreeable to the change and also believed, as I did, that Rodney was a good choice for my replacement.

The other basis for my giving up the chief role was the fact that since 2003, our medical center had been seeking a designation as a level two trauma center, and things were really starting to heat up. It was a competitive process with another medical center located about half a mile from our facility, and we were going through a lot of political battling and maneuvering as we prepared a proposal to present to the Sacramento county board of supervisors, the agency that would make the decision and award the nomination for trauma center status. Most of my work time was spent writing and editing the proposal, which needed to follow a format dictated by the request for proposals (RFP) issued by the county. I can't even begin to estimate the hours invested in the proposal by me; Rich; and Christy, our new RN trauma program manager we had hired in the summer of 2006. Christy had started four other trauma programs in her career, so she was extremely knowledgeable and invaluable in the entire process.

The hearing before the county supervisors had been delayed from July 2007 until the end of the year. In May, the proposals had both been submitted from the other medical center and us, and the process involved the director of health and human services reviewing both in great detail and then issuing a recommendation to the board of supervisors as to which medical center was most qualified and prepared to manage trauma services in the South Sacramento area. We felt confident that our hospital, by far, had the best staff, resources, and dedication to manage a trauma program. We also had complete support of our regional leadership in Oakland, something I had worked on since 2003 when we first discussed the possibility of becoming a trauma center.

As expected, after reviewing both proposals in detail and obtaining a recommendation from a team of trauma surgeons from the American College of Surgeons' Committee on Trauma (ACS—COT), the director of health and human services issued a statement of support for Kaiser and made a formal recommendation to the county board of supervisors to choose our medical center over the competition. The battle wasn't over, however; and it would drag out until the end of the year, when the final hearing was held.

A FRIEND IN HEAVEN

In January 2007, I had left work early to drop by the driving range and hit some golf balls. Suddenly, my cell phone rang and I answered it as I pulled into a parking place at the golf course.

"Mike?" Susan asked into her phone.

I could tell something was wrong, and she sounded like she had been crying. "What's wrong?" I shot back as my heart began to pound.

Susan answered back, "What are you doing? I just got a phone call from Bobby, Carol's son. She's had a massive bleed in her brain."

As I fought back tears, I told her where I was and asked if Carol had died. Susan explained that she was in the ICU on life support but things didn't look too good according to Bobby.

"I'm on my way home right now. Start packing a suitcase and we'll leave for San Diego as soon as possible," I shot back to her.

After we had moved to Davis, although we didn't see them as often, Susan and I kept in regular touch with Carol and Bob. After all, they were the Godparents of Christy, and Carol had been Susan's closest friend while we had our children and went through the surgeries with Christy. Susan and I were the Godparents for Megan, their youngest daughter. When I started medical school, Carol, Mandy, and Megan drove up to see us in Davis. I took them over to the medical school and showed Carol and Mandy our cadaver in the gross anatomy lab.

I was stunned by this news. Carol had always been the stalwart in our life and never said no to a request for help or advice. She ran her own hair salon that Bob had installed in their garage and acted not only as a hairstylist but also as a confidante and counselor to her customers. She babysat both David and Christy for us when Susan was working part—time in my Aunt Greta's escrow business, and our families did a lot of camping together through the years.

We left as soon as we could that afternoon and drove down to Santa Clarita, just north of LA. I was exhausted, and Susan has a difficult time driving at night. We spent the night in a motel and left early in the morning to get through LA and to San Diego.

Arriving around 11:00 a.m. at the hospital to which Carol had been transported two nights before, we found her room in the ICU. As we entered the room, she was sitting up in the bed, intubated but appearing to recognize us. She was surrounded by Bob, Bobby, Mandy, and Megan, her entire family, who all hugged us as we arrived. I was really surprised at how responsive she appeared, and the girls said she had been communicating with them by squeezing their hands to indicate yes or no. Apparently, the first night, the neurosurgeon told Bob that she most likely would not survive this bleed. It was at the base of the brain and brainstem, and this is a devastating location to have a large hemorrhage. However, after the first twenty—four hours, she was improving and was at the level of responsiveness we were seeing. The doctor offered them cautious optimism but warned that she wasn't out of the woods. We went with the kids, although they are all grown adults with Bobby and Mandy both married and with children of their own, into a quiet room to talk further while Bob stayed at Carol's side. Bobby suggested that we all pray together, so we joined hands and said the Our Father as a group.

With Carol's improved status, the neurosurgeon wanted to transfer her to Scripps Hospital in La Jolla so a cerebral angiogram could be performed to assess where the bleed originated and possibly occlude the site with a coil that blocks the vessel or aneurysm that bled. The first hospital she was taken to by the paramedics didn't have an angio suite or the capability to perform such a complicated procedure.

She was transferred that evening, and a neurointerventionalist was called in to perform the study. This is a very specialized radiologist who focuses on imaging the vessels in the brain and doing the coil procedure if possible. When he finished, he came to talk to the family along with Susan and me. He had found that all of the vessels in Carol's posterior circulation were twisted and narrowed, and he was unable to thread a catheter into them to localize the bleeding site. This was a congenital abnormality that occurs primarily in women and usually causes their death by the early twenties. Carol had been very fortunate to give birth to three children and live as long as she had, given the circumstances. Worse yet, she was developing vasospasm. This is a process where the blood vessels constrict in an effort to halt any further bleeding, but it actually worsens the damage by cutting off blood flow to the injured brain. They were giving her specialized medication to try to reverse the vasospasm, but the outcome looked ominous.

We had to leave and return to Northern California when my mother called to tell us my Dad was in the hospital after suffering a heart attack. We drove most of the night and finished the next morning, going straight to the hospital where Dad was staying in the cardiac care unit. He was doing much better, and the plan was to manage him with medications and not perform any interventions at that time.

He went home in a couple of days without any complications.

One week later, we returned to San Diego to be with Carol and her family. We took Christy with us on this trip, as the news was that Carol was worsening. Christy needed to have the opportunity to say good—bye to her Godmother, and we wanted to be with Carol one more time.

The morning we arrived, Susan and I got to the hospital before the family and I went into the ICU to Carol's side. She was beginning to have seizures and autonomic instability. This is a process that occurs as the brain is dying, and is characterized by the body temperature becoming erratic, normal electrolytes in the body becoming abnormal, and brain function and reflexes declining. The neurosurgeon stopped in while I was at her side and told me she was essentially brain dead and recovery would not happen. I whispered in Carol's ear, just on the outside chance she might be hearing and processing some sounds. I told her how much Susan and I loved her and that she needed to guide Bob and her children as to what they needed to do. If she was going to recover, show them a clear sign; if not, then let go and slip into heaven so their pain and anguish could start to heal.

Carol's body hung on for almost another week, and Bob was able to get her transferred to UC San Diego Medical Center for another opinion before they withdrew life support. This was so important to Bob, as he needed to know for sure that there was no hope of her recovery. When the family was ready, Carol was extubated and placed on comfort care and her body was allowed to begin the dying process. It took about three days for her to die peacefully with all of her family at her side.

We had returned home before she went to UCSD, and Bob called us the evening she passed. We returned to San Diego to attend her memorial mass at their Catholic parish in Scripps Ranch. It was a beautiful, loving mass, and we were honored to bring the gifts of bread and wine to the altar as a family. Susan and I also served as Eucharistic ministers, dispensing the body of Christ during communion. Many longtime, old friends were in attendance, some that we hadn't seen in over twenty years. Everyone there was present to pay tribute to one of the sweetest, loving, and giving friends that any of us had ever known in our lives. She was an angel in heaven now, watching over all of her earthly family.

ALOHA ON MY MIND

Susan and I both love Hawaii and Kauai in particular. It is the oldest of the islands, the first one to rise as an active volcano from the middle of the Pacific Ocean. Consequently, the island is very lush and tropical in most parts of it, and Mount Wai'ale'ale, the dormant crater, is the rainiest place on earth. On one trip to the island, we took a helicopter ride into the remnants of the crater and saw spectacular, ribbonlike waterfalls cascading down the sheer vertical cliffs. The top of the mountain is so wet that it is a swamp called the Alaka'i swamp and can only be accessed by a network of wooden trails over the wetlands. The area receives an incredible average of 430 inches per year of rainfall, hence the designation as the rainiest place on earth.

From 2005 on, we had taken annual trips to Kauai and stayed in a beautiful new condominium purchased by one of my fellow emergency physicians. I had hired him several years before, and I think he felt obligated to allow us to use the condo without charge. In recent years, it had become an annual destination for us, and we planned a two—week trip in October/November of 2007 while we awaited the December hearing with the county supervisors.

Just before our trip, I had noticed some minor, vague symptoms of lightheadedness when I bent over, such as picking up a golf ball from the cup. It bothered me very little, but a pediatrician colleague, who was also on part—time disability from a bout with leukemia, had advised that I tell my oncologists any and all symptoms I noticed. He had recently started a battle with the disability insurance carrier over their refusal to continue his partial disability coverage, saying they had video surveillance of him doing strenuous physical activities. He recommended that I keep a record of every post—treatment symptom and tell my physicians. At an early October appointment with my radiation oncologist, I casually mentioned the lightheadedness, and she recommended that we perform a brain MRI scan. She said it would more than likely be normal, but she had seen lung cancer patients with vague symptoms such as mine end up having brain metastases. I scheduled the MRI for the Monday evening after the weekend we returned from our Kauai trip.

Kauai was paradise, as usual, and was a great place to relax after all the stress of the trauma center political battle. The first week, our friends, Gail and Larry, joined us in the second bedroom of the condo, and our kids and their spouses came for the second week. We hiked, biked, snorkeled, kayaked, and even jumped off Kipu'u Falls, a hidden 20—foot waterfall that filled a large swimming area with rope swings out over the water. I felt so good, physically and mentally, and didn't even give a second thought to the upcoming MRI scan. After all, my oncologist expected it to be normal since I had no headaches, difficulty with speech, or imbalance while walking.

We flew back on the weekend before the Monday evening MRI appointment and unpacked our bags. I went into work during the day on Monday and then registered in radiology for the 5:15 p.m. scan. It had been eighteen years since I had last undergone a brain MRI, a scan that was done to assess my base—of—tongue tumor in 1989. The technician had me remove all metal, such as my watch, cell phone, badge, keys, and belt. She forgot, however, to tell me to remove my wallet. As I discovered about a week after the scan, all of my credit cards were demagnetized while I was in the scanner and had to be replaced by the issuing companies.

I lay in the tube for the twenty—five—to—thirty—minute scan, thinking back on how wonderful our Kauai trip had been and how good I felt physically. I felt as though I was finally back to normal after the chemotherapy and radiation treatment from my lung cancer.

When the scan was completed, I put my accessories back on and the technician said the reading radiologist wanted me to come down to her office.

Odd, I thought to myself, but maybe she wants to let me know it was negative so I won't worry until it is formally read.

When I entered her office, she asked me what kind of symptoms I had been experiencing that initiated the ordering of the MRI.

This isn't good, I thought, and told her it was just mild, occasional lightheadedness.

"Well," she started, "you have a mass in your posterior left hemisphere that is about three centimeters in diameter. Have you been having any headaches or visual disturbances?"

"No," I replied and then asked if it could be something other than a cancer metastasis.

"Well, it doesn't have the typical appearance of a brain met from your lung cancer, as the mass is very well encapsulated and there is little or no inflammation surrounding it. It could be an abscess. Have you been on any chronic steroid treatment?"

I told her that I had during my chemotherapy treatments in the prior year. My hope was buoyed by the thought that it might be something other than a brain metastasis, but my common sense was telling me to be ready for the worst. Brain mets after primary lung cancer are a common location for the cancer to spread, along with the bones, liver, and spleen.

I thanked the radiologist after she had gone over the images with me and made my way home to break the news to Susan and the family. After telling her the ominous news and both of us sharing tears together, I put a call into Mark Hawk, our chief of neurosurgery. Mark and I had been working closely together on building our case for the trauma center designation, and neurosurgery is a vital part of any trauma center. The number one cause of death in trauma victims is head injury. I reached Mark at home on his cell phone and told him the reason for the call. He pulled up the scan on his home computer, a wonderful tool that is part of the Kaiser electronic medical record system, HealthConnect. Mark looked at the scan and the large mass in the left hemisphere and matter—of—factly stated that it had to come out via surgery. Asking what if it was an abscess and not a met, he replied that it still had to be removed before any adjunctive therapy was initiated. Looking at his schedule, he asked if I wanted to have the surgery the next day. He had some free time in the late morning and could get me added onto the OR schedule as an emergency.

I was taken aback by how quickly it could be done, but after discussing it in thirty seconds with Susan, we both felt that the sooner it was done the better since we would just worry up to the time of the operation. I told Mark it was a go, and he asked me to come into the hospital that night for a mapping MRI scan and placement of markers on my scalp to help with intraoperative localization of the mass and minimize the loss of normal brain tissue during the resection of the tumor.

As Susan drove to the hospital, I began the difficult task of calling our children, my mother, and few close friends to let them know what was happening to me. Everybody was extremely shocked, but I was able to help calm them and let them know that my life and future were both in the hands of God and nothing could be gained by worrying about it. We checked into the Sacramento Kaiser hospital, which was where the neurosurgery service was based. Mark met us there and began getting me admitted and writing orders for an MRI that night. After the MRI, he came into my ICU room and began placing ten to twelve plastic markers that would show up on an MRI scan in the morning and remain in place during the operation. The markers would be used to localize the tumor using a STEALTH system. It's a patented computerized neuro—localization system for brain tumors. The system would provide computerized guidance as Mark and the assistant neurosurgeon opened my scalp, took out a piece of my skull over the site, and entered the brain tissue to expose the tumor. Mark had warned me that, due to the close proximity to my left occipital lobe, I might end up with some visual field deficits. I reassured him by saying he should do whatever he needed to do to get the entire tumor and I would deal with the aftereffects later.

When he met with me to talk about the next day's surgery, I asked Mark if this metastasis was the ominous beginning of the end. His reply was that it certainly wasn't a good thing to have but that many patients with brain metastases who underwent surgical removal followed by whole brain radiation were able to gain months and even up to an extra year from the treatments. I thanked him for the frank information and then thought how God had always brought me through incredible illnesses and given me more years on earth. Maybe this was another opportunity to demonstrate his incredible power to cure and use me as an example for those who met me. I was at peace with whatever his will would be; and if the brain met was how I would die, I would face it with dignity and be an example for others.

When we had been in Kauai just a week before, David, Michelle, Christy, and Steve had rented an SUV to drive around the island. They were given a Jeep Commander, which was a huge SUV that seated all six of us for tours and drives around Kauai. One of the days, we all took the short flight back to Oahu, as none of the four kids had ever been to Pearl Harbor or seen the North Shore, arguably the Mecca of big wave surfing. Our rental car for the day was none other than a Jeep Commander.

Going into the operating room, Susan and the kids all gave me tearful kisses and hugs, and I told them I would be okay and see them when I woke up. Mark was there to help move me and said to the family that it was pretty straightforward and unless they ran into any unexpected complications, I should be finished in about three hours.

"Oh, come on, Mark!" I quipped. "It isn't brain surgery. Oh wait. I guess it is brain surgery."

The first thing I remembered waking up was sensing that the five of them were at my side, along with our friends, Gail and Larry. I couldn't grasp how they got to my side all the way from Southern California so quickly since I had just called them and told them the news early that morning, but I was too fuzzy from the anesthesia to ask or care.

I kept having dreams about the surf being very big on the North Shore and apparently kept saying, "Let's get up to Pipeline and go surfing."

I fell back to sleep until a male voice woke me saying, "Let's go, Doc. We're going for a ride."

My groggy reply was, "Are we taking the Jeep Commander?" which elicited a relieved round of laughter from everyone surrounding me.

The next day, when I was more awake, I heard the story of how Gail and Larry booked an early morning flight from San Diego to Sacramento to be with me for the surgery. Even though we lived so far apart, they had been our closest friends through our entire lives, and this was a strong example of that friendship. We had traveled together, supported each other through tough times, and shared our joys with one another.

Mark Hawk visited me that day and related how he was able to get good margins around the tumor and there didn't appear to be any spread from the main metastasis or evidence of other tumors. He also told me the pathology had shown the mass to be squamous cell carcinoma, the type of cancer of the primary lung tumor.

"Well," I told him, "I've got my battle laid out before me, and my plan is to win it, albeit with God's tremendous help."

Incredibly, I was able to go home just forty—eight hours after brain surgery and had no pain or side effects from the operation. Mark had checked my vision prior to me being discharged, and there was no evidence of any peripheral vision deficits. God had certainly guided Mark's expert hand and allowed him to excise the entire cancer without damaging my visual cortex or my speech center, also near the tumor bed.

This entire string of events in my cancer battle had all occurred in less than a week after our wonderful trip to Kauai and Oahu. Amazed as I was, I knew it was all part of God's plan in our life and was intended to give us strength and faith in facing the battle ahead. The hardest fight was coming soon: whole brain radiation.

THE BLUE LIGHT

Whole brain radiation can be an incredible insult to the normal neu-rons and white matter of the human brain. It's a treatment that is used as a last resort for usually widespread cancer that has invaded the cen-tral nervous system. The treatment is normally considered palliative, an attempt to buy a little more time for those patients who will face their death in a year or less. While they never said this to me, I suspected this was the expectation of my oncologists. Their recommendations had been to enjoy what life I had left with my family and friends. They both strongly advised that I quit work and go out on full medical disability.

What neither of them was aware of was the incredible personal rela-tionship and guidance I had throughout all of my life from God. I knew I had to be spiritually ready to leave if it was God's will, but I equally had to be ready to go on living if that was where He led me. I resolved in my heart that I would accept either outcome and that every day I woke up I would thank my Creator for another day of life and precious time with my loving wife and children.

The first day of radiation, there were no alignment tattoos placed as there had been for my head and neck cancer and the primary lung cancer. A plastic mask was molded to my face and forehead that kept my head aligned with the radiation tube as the tube rotated around my skull from right to left. When the first treatment started, I was distinctly aware of a blue light that seemed to fill the room and continued until the thirty—second delivery of alpha particles to my brain was over. I thought that maybe they had added a blue laser to the linear accelerator to guide the treatments. I asked the technician if this was the case and described the blue light to her.

She said, "Just a minute. I want you to describe that to my co—worker."

She brought him into the room, and I recounted my story of the blue light.

"That's amazing!" he replied.

The senior technician then explained to me how, as the radiation passed through my brain and head, it stimulated the optic nerves going to my eyes. It was very common for patients to say they saw a blue light while being radiated, as the wavelength of the beam was in the blue end of the spectrum. She had just been describing this phenomenon to the junior technician who had never heard of it before; hence, his amazement that I described it after my treatment.

I also noticed the ozone smell of impending rain during each treatment. I asked the technician about this also, and she explained that the alpha particles reacted with the oxygen around my head and in my nose to create ozone. That was why I smelled it with each treatment.

With each treatment, I would spend the thirty to sixty seconds praying that God would let the radiation kill any cancer cells that might remain in my brain and spare the normal brain cells much damage. I was able to drive myself to each of the treatments but would need to sit in the car before starting to drive home, as the radiation made me feel odd in a way I can't really describe. The closest I can come to relating in words the way I felt is as though I had been hit in the head and neck without any severe pain but heaviness with associated nausea. Two thirds of the way through the course of radiation, I still had most of my normal hair; but when I started losing it, it occurred rapidly. It also seemed as though my scalp had been burned, with chunks of dry scalp coming off with hair follicles in it. I lost virtually all of my hair, except the very back of the scalp where my head laid on the plastic brace. To this day, I still have a patch on the back of my head that is darker and thicker than the rest of my scalp. It took much longer for my hair to regrow compared to when I lost it with chemotherapy, and it came back in very wispy and light—colored thin strands. My philosophy, however, has been that some hair is better than none at all and it's more important that I'm still alive.

After all the treatments end, there is always a letdown and the feeling that you are out on your own, just waiting for the next bit of bad news. During treatment of cancer, you can tend to focus on getting through the side effects and letting the treatment work to rid you of the malignancy. When it's all complete, you have to make a decision about where you go mentally. Do I live on a tenuous edge and let worry devour me thinking about the possible return of cancer? Or do I go on living, being thankful for the blessings I've had in my life and giving thanks for every extra day? I chose the latter attitude, since I believe that it is a better approach for my immune system and overall psyche. I've known friends in my life who have given up after getting a diagnosis of cancer and allowed themselves to become depressed and defeated. They might have died of their cancer anyway, but why help it consume you? The challenge for me has been to always try to be aware of God's plan for the remainder of my life and not to squander the gift of extra life.

THE GREATEST FAMILY BLESSING

In early June 2009, our daughter Christy came over in the afternoon on one of her days off from her nursing job. I heard her arrive as she pulled her car into the driveway while I was throwing a bag of trash into the can on the side of the garage. I came around into the garage to see her and Susan intense in conversation.

I walked up to them and asked, "What's up?"

Christy replied, "I have a present for you, Dad."

She pulled a plastic item out of her pocket and handed it to me. At first, I couldn't imagine what it was and why it was a gift for me. Then I saw a faint purple plus sign in a window at one end of it, and I realized I was looking at a positive pregnancy test.

"Oh, Christy," I said as I gave her a big hug, "you're making me cry." I realized I was going to become a grandfather.

"That's the reaction I was hoping to see from you, Mom," Christy stated.

Instead, when Susan received the news right before me, all she could say was an emphatic, "No!" It wasn't that she didn't want Christy to be pregnant with our first grandchild, but she was just stunned into disbelief when she saw the positive test.

Christy and Steve began the early pregnancy process of confirming the positive test and having blood tests drawn to check for things like blood type and Rh status, immunity to rubella, presence of any sexually transmitted diseases, and other basic screening labs. Christy had placed conception at right around Memorial Day at the end of May, so it would be another five to six weeks before she would have an ultrasound to confirm a live pregnancy.

Susan accompanied her to the first prenatal visit to get her into the system at Kaiser. Because of her history of a congenital heart defect and her multiple surgeries, she was stratified into the high—risk pregnancy group. After the visit, they stopped by my office, where I was working on some administrative tasks for the ER. They asked if I could do an ultrasound to look at the baby, and I was elated to do it. Our emergency physician group is very versed and well trained in bedside ultrasound, and we have no fewer than four ultrasound machines in the department. We found an empty room, and I grabbed an unused machine to take a quick look. We estimated she was about six weeks along, so I told her we should be able to see the pregnancy by an abdominal scan, but to see any detail, we would need to do a transvaginal scan.

She declined to have her dad do such an intimate exam, so I said, "Let's just see what we can see on your tummy."

I squirted gel on the transducer and placed it on her bare stomach. Sliding it down to the mid pelvis region, a very clear intrauterine pregnancy came into view. The strong heartbeat was visible as well as the embryo moving about frequently. This simple ultrasound reassured Christy that she had a living, active baby in her body.

Even though it was before her scheduled formal ultrasound at eighteen to nineteen weeks, Christy and Susan came by my office after her routine sixteen—week appointment and asked if I would do another ultrasound. Christy really wanted to know the sex if we were able to determine it. I did the abdominal scan, and it appeared there was a small stub in between the legs of the baby, and I showed it to Christy and Susan. They were both elated that it might be a boy but said that Steve would be slightly disappointed when he came home from work and heard the results of the scan. He had really set his desires on having a little girl. However, he would still be happy and just wanted a healthy baby. I cautioned them that it was very early in the pregnancy and the future formal ultrasound in radiology would give us better confirmation on the sex of the baby.

Christy's pregnancy progressed normally, and by the time she was twenty weeks along, the baby had been definitively identified as a boy. More importantly, an intrauterine echocardiogram had also been performed, and the neonatologist who did the exam told Christy that he was 100 percent certain there were no congenital defects with the baby. Normally, he couldn't say with 100 percent certainty, but since Christy was so small and thin, he could conclusively make this statement.

At about twenty—seven to twenty—eight weeks, Christy began having pre—term contractions. An exam was done by her high—risk OB—GYN, and it confirmed she was in labor, with her cervix dilated 1 cm. She spent two nights in the hospital for monitoring and then was sent home on strict bed rest. Christy was extremely bored but worried as she continued to have contractions. Susan would go to her house when Steve was at work, and they would often lie in bed together and watch movies on DVDs. Alex, her OB—GYN, wanted to get her to at least thirty—five weeks. The whole bed rest ended up being almost two months of her pregnancy.

At her thirty— five—week checkup with Alex, he told Christy she was still in early labor but could now get up and be active within safe limits. This meant no bungee jumping, roller skating, or other crazy activities, but exercise, walks, and shopping were all approved. If she went into full—blown, active labor, it would be fine, as the baby's lungs were mature and he should do well postpartum.

A few days later, Christy and Steve announced that they had decided on their son's name. It would be Noah Michael, which was a humbling honor for me to know he carried my name as his middle moniker.

Christy did well the next couple of weeks and then called me on the Sunday of the thirty—seventh week and said she was having severe pains in her lower chest/upper abdomen. I told her she should go to the hospital to get checked and maybe get an EKG done to make sure her heart was fine. After a couple of hours, she called us at home to let us know she was being admitted as she was in active labor. The pains she had been having were actually strong contractions radiating into her chest.

Alex, her doctor, just happened to be on duty and told her, "Let's have a baby today."

Christy was being followed in the high—risk pregnancy program at Kaiser Hospital in Roseville, CA. This was about a forty—five—minute drive from our home in Davis, so we jumped in the car and began the anxious trek to be at her side. We arrived at the labor and delivery area just as she was being roomed and hooked up to the monitors. She was in good spirits but starting to feel the contractions increase in their intensity. As the nurse, a friend of hers from nursing school, just got the monitors completely hooked up, Christy went into a massive contraction that wasn't relaxing. The monitor was off the scale, but more concerning was that the baby's heart rate was dropping. The nurse called the desk for Alex to come in; and as he arrived, the baby's heart rate steadily dropped from a normal 120 beats per minute down to 54 beats per minute. When Alex saw this, he quickly told the nurse to call a Code C, which means an emergency Caesarian section. He grabbed the end of her gurney and began pulling her out of the room as the monitors were yanked loose from the wall. I ran to Christy's side as she rolled toward the door and saw an old familiar look of fear and uncertainty in her eyes that harkened back to taking her to the OR for her open—heart surgeries. I told her as I patted her hand that everything was going to be okay. I could tell by the look she was giving me that she was having a hard time believing it.

As we saw her roll away, I grabbed Susan as we both began to cry. Noticing that Steve too was starting to cry, we enveloped him with our arms and we began to pray together. I could tell how worried he was not only about his baby son but also about his wife.

"Heavenly Father," I prayed for all of us, "we are not worthy to receive you, but please send your Holy Spirit to protect both Christy and Noah. We have faith that you can and will make everything all right as I told Christy when she left us."

Just then, one of Christy's best friends, Sarah, walked into the room and quickly asked what was happening. She had arrived in the lobby just as the overhead operator's message about a Code C began to repeatedly be broadcast throughout the hospital. We quickly updated Sarah, even though we had not heard the status of either Christy or Noah. Alex came into the room after about five minutes since he had hustled the gurney out of the room with our daughter and grandson being rushed into the OR in labor and delivery. Four very anxious and tearful family members and friends looked at him with great anticipation as he informed us that mom and baby were both doing well. He recounted that as soon as they got her into the OR, the massive contraction relaxed and the baby's heart rate started rising. However, as soon as her uterus started another contraction, it dropped back into the fifties and the anesthesiologist gassed her down for the emergency C—section. When they got Noah out, they found that his umbilical cord was a double nuchal cord; that is, it was wrapped twice around his neck. It also looped through his legs before attaching to his umbilicus. He never would have made it down the birth canal if Christy had progressed toward a vaginal delivery. Alex was able to get him out in less than five minutes, and his Apgar scores were 8 and 9, very good for a newborn infant who had just gone through what our Noah had experienced.

Breathing sighs of relief all around, Steve started saying out loud, "Thank you, God! Thank you so much! You are so unbelievably powerful. You saved my wife and my baby boy."

It was the most spiritual of moments as the four of us gave thanks and praise, and it was the most outward expression of faith I had ever seen from Steve.

I could tell that something concerned Alex as he first rushed back into the room and he looked kind of pale. After things had calmed down a little, he told us, "I am so grateful that I was on call today. If it had been anybody else, they probably would have sent Christy home since she hadn't dilated very much and wasn't having regular, frequent contractions when we first checked her. If she had gone home and suffered that massive contraction at home, we would have lost Noah and possibly even Christy."

I felt myself shaking inside as I heard Alex's words and knew, with no doubt, that it was the hand of God that put this whole day in motion.

Steve was the first one to see and hold his beautiful new son. Christy was still in the OR as the resident physician closed her incision, and all of us got to see Noah ahead of her. Steve's parents, Jackie and Lynn, arrived as we were going into the recovery room to see Noah. We all took turns going in to be with Steve as he held this wonderful new infant and could easily see the relief and pride on his face. When Christy came into the recovery room from the OR, we all stepped out so they could have some private family and bonding time. Christy immediately began breastfeeding Noah, but it was difficult, as she was so drowsy from the anesthesia.

When I got the chance to go in with Christy, I told her how much I loved her but told her, more importantly, how much God loves her and had watched over her and Noah during this crisis. I asked her if she remembered looking into my eyes as I told her everything would be all right.

And she replied, "Oh yes, Dad, I remember. I also hoped that I would be asleep before they cut into my abdomen. I was awake while they hurriedly prepped and draped me and saw Alex pick up the scalpel before it all went black. My last thought was that I was either going to wake up with a new baby or with the news that he had died."

I gave her a tearful hug and told her that God never would have allowed such a beautiful creation to die right after he was born. Noah was a fantastic blessing on our entire family and, with God watching over him, would be part of it for a long, long time.

EPILOGUE

As you now know from the previous chapters, God has been an integral part of our lives since we were born. Sometimes we forget that basic fact, but there is always something that quickly reminds us that He is there and guiding our lives. It might be something that is tragic or joyful, but we can never forget that He is the light, the truth, and the way that watches over us.

One morning, I woke up early, around 5:00 a.m. I was reflecting on where my life had been and where it was now heading. Throughout the years, when we would share with friends or acquaintances one or several of our stories from our life together, it would usually lead to telling people about Susan's tremendous conversion experience or our experiences with devastating illness or how hard it was to take our daughter, Christy, through two temporary shunt operations and two open—heart corrections in her short lifetime. Amazingly, their response has always been the same: "Oh my gosh. You guys have been through so much in your lives. You need to write a book about it all." Well, that morning, at 5:00 a.m., I was overcome by the realization that they all were right and God was speaking to me through them. I began to think about how to frame the stories; which ones to include; and what, if any, should be left out. I made the commitment that if God would lead my words and show me what to write, I would promise to see the project through to the finish. That very day, I ordered a mini laptop computer so I could work on the stories anywhere, at any time I felt the Spirit guide me. I've written at home, on vacation trips, and even sitting at the beach in Southern California. At times, I've left the book for weeks at a time, but I always came back to my commitment with God.

We are now in 2011, and our journey isn't over. I have been in remission from cancer since I finished my treatments for the brain metastasis at the end of 2007. In November 2010, I was three years out from that tumor. And February 2011 was five years since my diagnosis with the primary lung cancer. I can only believe that God has much more for me to accomplish before I leave.

Christy, my tiny, blue baby whom we didn't know if she would survive to childhood, let alone to adulthood, is now thirty years old and a mommy to Noah. She got her nursing degree, followed by a master's of nursing education, and is working on a project with Kaiser— Permanente to develop an educational program for adults who were born with congenital heart defects. She works clinically in the pediatric intensive care unit in Kaiser Hospital Roseville, the same building where her frightening delivery of Noah occurred.

My hope is these written stories may touch a reader in a way that brings them back to a buried faith or sparks a desire in them to search for the reasons we exist and how we came to be created. What matters is that you recognize we didn't just randomly appear without any purpose for our existence and that death is just a door to eternity, whether it occurs early in our life here on earth or late in the lifetime of our human experience.

I know that for me, there is undoubtedly a Higher Power behind the grand creation of everything, from the endless galaxies and solar systems of the universe, down to the microcosm of molecules, atoms, and subatomic particles. That Higher Power is God, and knowing him will open your life and your soul to countless blessings in your existence. Sometimes we might not see illness, loss of a loved one, or financial difficulties as blessings; but if you search for the meaning of every event and remain open to the Holy Spirit, you will come to know the purpose of those events. It might sound strange, but I would never want to go back and avoid the hardships, bouts with cancer, and loss of beloved friends and family. Every event, good or bad, that has occurred in my life has happened for a reason; and it usually bestows wisdom, humility, and awe of God on me when I pray for the understanding of each one.

God might be touching you through others around you, an illness, or the death of a loved one. You might find Him in the world and nature surrounding you, in a church or hospital, or even in your own home. Wherever it might be, be sure to open your heart and soul and you will be filled with endless grace and countless blessings. I know that I have found God in many events and places throughout my life. These blessings of a faithful man and the loving family and friends who have been there in my lifetime will last for eternity.